Farewell to Democracy?

Lessons Past and Present

Jack Luzkow

Winchester, UK
Washington, USA

JOHN HUNT PUBLISHING

First published by Zero Books, 2021
Zero Books is an imprint of John Hunt Publishing Ltd., No. 3 East St., Alresford,
Hampshire SO24 9EE, UK
office@jhpbooks.com
www.johnhuntpublishing.com
www.zero-books.net

For distributor details and how to order please visit the 'Ordering' section on our website.

Text copyright: Jack Luzkow 2020

ISBN: 978 1 78904 166 8
978 1 78904 167 5 (ebook)
Library of Congress Control Number: 2020934414

A CIP catalogue record for this book is available from the British Library.

Design: Stuart Davies

UK: Printed and bound by CPI Group (UK) Ltd, Croydon, CR0 4YY
Printed in North America by CPI GPS partners

We operate a distinctive and ethical publishing philosophy in
all areas of our business, from our global network of authors to
production and worldwide distribution.

Contents

Introduction

History and Democracy

In 1989 we heard that history had ended. Liberal democracy had won the Cold War and become the only legitimate story. Communism and fascism were now permanently discredited relics of the past. Democracy was now heralded as triumphant. Soon it would be global, spanning all continents.

Fascism had been based on fear, hatred, and division. It embraced tyranny. And it led to war, and then genocide. By 1945 fascism was a brutal memory, it no longer was a guidepost to humanity's future: it had never been. It was a past that had passed.

By 1989 Soviet communism had also failed. It simply rotted from within. It had failed to develop an economic model that could compete with the West. It had preserved class struggle: capitalist bosses were replaced by commissars. It had led to a different kind of genocide and to imperial wars. It had been unable to solve social inequality. It had created new elites. It had been no kinder to minorities. It had failed to modernize or to build the utopia that it had promised. By 1989 it had ceased to be a story with a future. Nobody believed in it.

The only story still standing after 1989 (hypothetically), the only credible narrative was liberal democracy. It was a story that virtually all political parties in the West embraced: civil liberties, the freedom of movement of goods, ideas, and individuals, political rights. The liberal-democratic story achieved a broad consensus. The past had been a closed society, earlier regimes had suppressed personal liberties, denied free markets, curtailed freedoms of expression and access to (alternative) ideas, suppressed political choice. For most of history few people voted, there was no constitution, political power was

1

restricted to an elite few, and personal liberties were limited to the fortunate and the affluent. For most of history "information" was closely guarded and kept secret by the elect few, wealth was concentrated at the top, and both liberty and equality seemed a utopian dream at best.

The liberal-democratic story claimed to change all that. The freedom of movement for people, ideas, goods, and capital would be a great equalizer. Political rights were universal, everybody who was a citizen voted. People were citizens, not subjects. Citizens had personal rights and civil liberties and a constitution that supported them. Liberty was joined by the free market, the open society, political equality. And government was not opaque.

After World War II, Western countries in particular added social and economic equality (social democracy). The state had a prophylactic role in the social and economic welfare of its citizens. Democracy could not thrive in unequal countries: war and depression proved that. Liberty was meaningless if surrounded by poverty. The free movement of goods meant little if there was too much joblessness. Political rights and democracy could not be sustained in the midst of racial and minority exclusions and animosities. And destabilized democracies would surely lead to demagogues.

Democratic regimes meant that people thought for themselves, they were responsible for their own histories. Democratic regimes meant access to education where citizens learned they had rights and the power to determine their fates. Democracy meant rejecting political demagogues, bigoted priests, and self-appointed soothsayers. The democratic story was celebrated as the last and inevitable story after the collapse of alternatives. Barack Obama certainly believed it. So did many Republicans before and even today.

Circa 1975, the "liberal" democratic story was joined by the globalization story. Globalization would lift all boats. Free markets and free trade would benefit all nations. Liberalization and globalization together would mean eternal progress. Open societies and open economies would mean prosperity and peace at last. No more closed societies, no more walls or barbed-wire fences: only open borders, common markets, free trade, and the unleashing of capital. All countries were invited to hold these "simple truths."

After 1989, virtually all nations that had been in the Soviet orbit, including Poland, Hungary, and Czechoslovakia, opted for the new democratic "religion." They embraced free trade, open borders, civil society, and globalization. Political rights, personal liberties, and democracy were touted as roads to the future. There were celebrations. At last there was a future. A new global order was emerging, and it was good. China remained a thriving outcast, but it was sure to fail.

By 1989 it did seem that the end of history had come. The future could offer nothing new, only more of the present. There were no alternatives, all that needed to be done was to perfect the institutions that already existed. The American version of the end of history was elegant and simple. The Industrial Revolution was part of a Natural Order that gave birth to a market, which provided a foundation for Democracy, which led inevitably to Globalization, which produced Universal Happiness.

In the European story, History produced the Nation, the Nation inevitably led to Nationalism, and Nationalism led to war. So Europe chose a new path toward peace and integration: Europeans had no doubt that integration meant human rights and the sanctity of the individual. The European Union was the antidote to Nationalism, it signified no borders, prophylactic states, perfect and Universal Happiness.

Then came the Russian story. Until the collapse of the Soviet Union in 1991, this narrative was rooted in communist ideology: Nature created Technology, Technology created Social Classes, Social Classes led to Revolution, which led to Utopia, which led to Universal Happiness.

It was the collapse of this latter version of Utopia that led to celebrations of the end of history across America and Europe. The failure of the Soviet Utopia was a *cause celebre* for the victory of market capitalism and liberal democracy. The new millennial order was celebrated in Europe as well: Europeans busied themselves forming the European Union even as the corpse of the Soviet Union was still smoldering. Concealed in all these expectations of the end of history was the disappearance of history itself. Each of the three stories had been based on the politics of inevitability, on mythologies or ideologies that had nothing to do with history: each branded a new religion, a new story of redemption, a new emancipation of humanity. And each was entirely wrong.

The Soviet story was the first to collapse. This story ran straight into history and facts. Instead of a democratic communist utopia, the return of history meant secession states locked into disputes over borders, ancient faiths on a permanent collision course, a new class of billionaire oligarchs that monopolized much of the wealth in Russia, a kleptocracy instead of a communist Commonwealth of equals, an authoritarian plutocracy more akin to proto-fascism of the 1930s than an "end of history."

And that was not all. Russian history post-1991 — the same for the history of Ukraine post-1991 — was proof that the American version of past and future was wrong: "nature" does not lead to the "market," does not lead to "democracy," does not lead to "happiness." The attempt of America to transplant itself into Russia was a monumental failure — as any sober analysis would have concluded. And that failure would have ramifications. Vladimir Putin would reply in kind. He attempted to transplant Russia into America, and he achieved a success that even he could not have predicted. But American confusion was not only the result of Putin's counter-insurgency: it was based on the illusion that American exceptionalism had triumphed in 1991, and that the entire world would follow its lead — voluntarily or not.

But one hardly needed to go to Russia to learn that American triumphalism was only so much blather rooted in a gigantic myth about itself and the universality of its own story. One could just as easily travel to Michigan or Oho or Pennsylvania or Wisconsin and many other states and learn the same thing: the future was winding down even as the celebration continued. The American led invasion of Iraq in 2003, which led to a disastrous meltdown of much of the Middle East, was a sign of what could happen when myth replaced history and facts. And then came another sign: the 2008 financial meltdown in the United States contradicted the so-called magical powers of the market. Combined with the 2010 deregulation of political campaign contributions, the power of the ultra-wealthy and of corporate America was magnified, even as the power of voters (and democracy) was diminished. America's future as universal paradigm was no longer assured. American mythology had run straight into history, and facticity, and lost. Instead of a straight line into the future, instead of certainty that nature provided for free markets that led to Democracy that led to Happiness, America now fastened on its victimhood, on its past and how to Make America Great Again. America was retrofitted for nationalism. It looked to the past, not the future.

After 2008 at the latest, Americans no longer believed that the future was on their side. They experienced unprecedented inequality. They lost their jobs and their homes by the millions. They no longer had a functional state. Health care, education, social security were at risk, no longer as assured as before. Technology, long heralded as guaranteeing a better future for all of us, now eliminated our jobs, even as it also poisoned the planet. Human wisdom, which might have seemed inexhaustible, now seemed finite and flawed. Infinite progress now dissolved into meaningless excess. Self-confidence eroded into emptiness.

Today, Liberal Democracy is in crisis throughout much of the West. There is no indication that it is victorious elsewhere or anywhere. China has not collapsed, not a few see it as the future (it won't be) and many have begun to think that China is on the right side of history (despite Hong Kong). The global financial crisis of 2008 was followed by challenges to the liberal-democratic story throughout much of the West. From the US to Eastern Europe there has been a resurgence of walls, rejection of immigrants, oppression of minorities, the emergence of authoritarian polities, divisions in the EU, exit from the EU by Britain, the demeaning of democracy (illiberal democracies) in countries as diverse as Brazil, Hungary, Poland, Russia, Turkey, the UK, and the US. Massive inequalities have reappeared, especially in the US and UK. And a trade war with China is still heating up.

Globalization has not been the panacea that was advertised. Globalization has wreaked havoc on the planet by promoting growth before we are able to harness that growth safely and ecologically. It has put pressure on the planet that is not sustainable. It has coincided with wars that are the result of ecological catastrophes, also caused by unsustainable growth. Wars have led to massive in-migration from the Middle East and destabilized many European nations.

The US has helped discredit the liberal-democratic story. Within the last few decades it has attempted to install democracy in Iraq and Libya at gunpoint, as it had attempted to do earlier in Vietnam. It has produced unprecedented inequality at home. It has shredded the social safety net. It has given tax breaks to the rich at the expense of all others. No wonder that people in West Virginia, and Kentucky, the Dakotas and Montana, from Kansas and Nebraska to Texas have rejected liberalism (and democracy) as undesirable: instead, they have embraced their racial and national and even their gender privileges. They prefer the hierarchical world in which their place is assured.

Others have come to see that liberalization and globalization are systems or covers that empower a global elite while depriving everybody else of the gains enriching that elite. The victory of Donald Trump is a direct result of this massive rejection of the liberal-democratic story. So is Brexit in the UK.

The liberal-democratic story survived two world wars. It came out of World War II as the dominant story. It stood for freedom and democracy. It gave up — or was forced to give up — colonialism. It organized the global order, and established the World Trade Organization (WTO) to manage it. It faced down Soviet communism. It led the Information and Cybernetic Revolution and it convinced much of the world that it should emulate the West. The liberal-democratic narrative, briefly, was triumphant: free markets and open borders led to prosperity, which led to democracy, which led to happiness. It was a virtuous circle, it was an eternal story. History ended — and moved into eternity.

Then came the counter-revolution. Vladimir Putin decided to resurrect Russian nationalism and empire: he saw the global order — led by the US — as a lance directed at him and Russia. Radical Islam kicked in with a glorious jihad (war) against the "materialist" West. Then China joined the WTO. China's mission was not to embrace liberalism, but rather to develop itself and to compete with the West. Receding now, because of all these challenges, was the myth of a global cornucopia. The globe was reverting to the past.

And then economic (neo)liberalism ran into more challenges that it helped to create. Unlimited trade and economic development threatened the planet. Free markets often turned into monopolies, and this in turn led to greater inequality. Abandoning (or diminishing) the social safety net, especially in the US and the UK, promised more instability. The cybernetic (digital) revolution promised progress, but it also produced joblessness. And more instability. And then the EU, a unified

Europe, began to unravel, challenged by migrants, nationalist ideology, pockets of anti-Semitism, and a fractious Britain. Everywhere the past was catching up to the present. Everywhere there was disillusionment about the future. Everywhere there was need for a new story. There were signs of a new story, but they were not comforting. We appeared to be cascading into an era of post-democracy: a period where the shell of democratic institutions endured, but mostly to be used by autocrats who used them to limit the freedoms won by centuries of struggle.

Chapter 1

Learn from the Past: Or Repeat It

Almost imperceptibly we have passed into an era of post-democracy. The courts are packed in order to promote a specific ideological agenda. A president calls for investigations into those investigating him for criminal or impeachable activities. Congress issues subpoenas that are rebuffed on the basis of executive privilege. A political party that is in the minority searches for ways to keep itself in power indefinitely by removing limits on campaign spending. Social media are used to generate alternative worlds and to draw us into those worlds to make us forget the world we are actually living in. A president espouses complete fictions, such as Ukrainian interference in the United States' elections of 2016, and his political party supports him in the face of all conflicting evidence.

As people have accommodated themselves to social media, and screens, and sound bites, they have lost their critical faculties. Words and sentences become clichés, vocabularies become diminished, concepts become more flattened and difficult to formulate, dissent less proclaimed, truth more orthodox — as if it is oracular in the mouths of would-be tyrants. People lose the habit of reading more reflective texts, and then lose the habit of reading altogether. Without an understanding of these phenomena, we fall into a trance, the victims of endless visual stimuli on our (television, phone, and computer) screens that transform us from citizens into consumers: politics becomes a kind of entertainment. Into this morass the past disappears altogether, it becomes whatever the loudest voice says it is. As memory of the past is debased, the present seems disconnected and future horizons vanish altogether.

During the interwar period, demagogues manipulated

the public through the tools of mass communication. They understood that people could be seduced by visual images that moved too rapidly for anybody to digest or to react critically to them. This contrasted with the printed word, which was read at the pace chosen by the reader. Books used larger vocabularies, they provided greater context, and reading was interactive.

Demagogues understood all of this instinctively. That was why they suppressed books, used the (movie) screen to fabricate myths and replaced complex ideas with simplified clichés. George Orwell, in his novel *1984* (1949), sounded a warning to the future. In *1984*, books are burned and people are controlled by a regime that monitors them through a two-way television screen. Language of the visual media is simplified while words are continually removed from the official dictionary. In Aldous Huxley's *Brave New World* (1932), the Controller of Western Europe conditions infants to avoid books: loud explosions occur whenever toddlers touch pages. The same Controller declares: "History is bunk." In *Brave New World*, there are no books nor is there a past. Only a campaign against the past; the closing of museums, the blowing up of historical monuments, the suppression of all books published before and even 150 years after the founding of the new regime. Christianity is gone, so is the soul, and so is "a thing called God." But without knowledge of the past, nobody notices.

The shrinking of vocabulary, the burning of books, the domination of the screen, the disappearance of history, the vanishing of alternative worlds and ideas, diminishes the ability to think abstractly and independently. It becomes more difficult to remember the past, to understand the present, or to explore wider visions for the future. Alternative lives — and alternative ideas — cannot be imagined; in Huxley's world independent thinking is vaporized by narcotics — until the present becomes "eternal." And the regime lives on forever since no opposition can be conceptualized and anyway it is futile.

Orwell and Huxley were describing a one-dimensional world in which all nuances of color and meaning had been flattened. They were anticipating the world of today: a world in which the words and language of the media, of the 24-hour news cycle, create a blur, a continual refocusing until they become the framework for our own language and thought. We become the mirror of what we hear and see, until we begin to mimic what comes through the screen because we lack the vocabulary and the concepts needed to make critical judgments: we lack a sense of the past to give us a context for the present. Demagogues don't need to burn books because we are increasingly immune or indifferent to the ideas within them. In a word, too many of us no longer read serious texts that help us get beyond the one-dimensional world that we have come to inhabit.

The Founding Fathers understood the importance of remembering and learning from history, from the texts that described and analyzed the past. Ancient Athens provided them with an invaluable lesson: it was there that popular (direct) democracy had descended into mob rule and tyranny. To avoid the fate of Athens, James Madison, in the *Federalist Papers*, advocated representative government. Otherwise the new republic was likely to descend "into factionalism, demagoguery, and then the seizure of power by some dictator to restore order." There was no cure, he added, "for the mischiefs of factionalism."

Plato, in *The Republic*, believed that popular democracy readily evolved into autocracy. People were ill equipped, he said, to select the best rulers and wisest courses of action. They so loved being flattered that they fell prey to unscrupulous flatterers.

Today, glib politicians use clichés, promote alternative facts, generate fictional narratives, and claim that criticism of them is unfair defamation of their character. They claim their critics are enemies of the people. They promote hatred of anybody who is an obstacle to their rise to power. They challenge truths that are uncomfortable for them. They make promises (jobs, walls, peace) they can't and won't keep. They threaten violence, promote fear of the "Other" and demonize vulnerable minorities. They stimulate mob action against perceived rivals, such as leaders of a rival political party or journalists writing in newspapers and magazines critical of them.

In the twenty-first century we are facing threats similar to totalitarianism in the twentieth century. Representative government no longer insulates elected leaders from the convulsions of people who can harass members of Congress around the clock online. Social media allows factions to form that become virtual mobs crossing virtual boundaries and intimidating opponents in the real world.

The current president exploits the mob mentality, which he helps to create. He uses social media to inflame public debates and to direct supporters to attack politicians who are critical of him. The president creates his own fake news and turns it into "instantaneous reality." His falsehoods are then retweeted by the virtual mob by the tens of thousands. "The real threat," says Anonymous in *The Warning*, "is when the madness bleeds over from the digital world into the real one, as it does at Trump events." Meanwhile, magical thinking is tweeted in an endless flow: Ukraine intervened in the US elections of 2016, not Russia; the president is a genius; the economy is better than ever (it is for some of us); immigrants are criminals. If they throw rocks, the president hints that they should be shot by our armed forces.

Back in the twentieth century, Friedrich Hayek, in *The Road to Serfdom*, noticed how authoritarian figures come to power. They exploit the more primitive instincts of people, especially those who are most vulnerable, "who have no strong convictions of their own but are ready to accept a ready-made system of values if it is only drummed into their ears sufficiently loudly and frequently." Autocrats appeal to basic human weaknesses. "It seems to be easier for people to agree on a negative program — on the hatred of an enemy, on the envy of the better off — than on any positive task. The contrast between 'we' and 'they' is consequently always employed by those who seek the allegiance of huge masses."

To manage the totalitarian state, Hayek observed, authoritarians blend the faithful together by appealing to basic human vulnerabilities. These true believers are prepared to accept "specious justification of vile deeds." But they must be willing to carry them out as well. "Since it is the supreme leader who alone determines the ends, his instruments must have no moral convictions of their own. They must, above all, be unreservedly committed to the person of the leader."

Not defending moral convictions of their own, people surrender themselves willingly. The president uses charged rhetoric to spur them on. He uses social media to inflame public debates. He urges the mob to attack his enemies (anybody opposed to him). The outcome is a virtual mob willing to use virtual weapons to assault real political opponents. The outcome is the death of truth amidst the endless tweeting of falsehoods.

The one advantage we have today is that we can learn from the totalitarian past. We know that people can be misled when information is concealed from them, or when truth and invention are deliberately blurred, as Orwell and Huxley understood. They also instructed us to beware of (representatives) politicians, who are often fellow travelers of autocrats. We have watched how eagerly members of Congress can line up behind demagogues; defending the president's thesis that Ukraine tampered in the US election of 2016; or insisting that the American president did not pressure the Ukrainian president to withhold military assistance in return for an investigation into his political rival.

We have to relearn the tools of democracy and the lessons of history. These have included citizens' initiatives that can put a referendum on the ballot: for example, a citizens movement in Missouri that succeeded in overturning a "right to work" law passed by the legislature. Such initiatives have succeeded in many other states as well. The lesson is that democracy works when we insist on acting as citizens and when we are knowledgeable about our own past (and present) and what we can accomplish simply by asserting rights that should inalienably be ours.

Chapter 2

The Power of the Powerless: We are Never Powerless

No matter how desperate, how isolated, how repressed we may feel, there has almost never been a period of history when at least some of us have not resisted. And just as often, many have resisted regimes they found repressive, even when those regimes perpetuated myths about their own legitimacy, or inevitability. Rebellion begins when myths are challenged, when "legitimacy" is demythologized. During World War II there was a myth that the German army was invincible. No army, let alone unarmed civilians, could possibly stand up to it. Yet it failed as early as December 1941 in the battle for Moscow. It failed in the battle for Britain. It failed in the battle for Stalingrad. It failed at the tank Battle of Kursk. And it continued to fail until the Russian army occupied Berlin and the Americans fought their way to the Elbe.

During the Holocaust, German Jews found themselves isolated, despised, and routinely interned in concentration and death camps. Jews living in Poland, after the German invasion in September 1939, and then the partition of Poland between Germany and Soviet Russia, were soon ghettoized and subsequently sent to camps, from Treblinka to Bergen-Belsen. Jews living in Soviet Russia, following the invasion of the German army, were slaughtered through the combined efforts of the German SS and the German army. Those not murdered at once were sent to ghettos, where they were penned in and starved. Survivors were sent to death camps, where they perished.

Yet even in these conditions, many resisted: they did not accept their fate as something irresistible or inevitable. On August 2, 1943, about 1000 Jewish prisoners at Treblinka death camp rebelled against their Nazi captors, with virtually no weapons other than the axes and small firearms they were able to take from their guards. On October 14, 1943, prisoners at Sobibor death camp rebelled and killed 14 SS and police auxiliaries, and then set the camp on fire. Some 300 prisoners escaped through the barbed wire and minefields surrounding the camp. Between 1941 and 1943, there were about 100 rebellions in ghettos across Eastern Europe. There was no single strategy, but there was a unifying aim: break out from the ghettos and join local partisan movements.

Inscribed on a marble memorial wall in Warsaw are names of perished Jews. They had been living in the Warsaw Ghetto, and this was the disembarkation point, for many, to the death camp Treblinka, a place where my grandfather's parents likely perished. By spring, April 1943, the population of the Warsaw Ghetto had dwindled to 50,000 (from a half million at the peak). By then residents were surrounded by a wall; they had little food, almost no weapons (except for what they had smuggled in), virtually no medicines, and they were isolated from the world from which they could expect little help. Yet the inhabitants of the Warsaw Ghetto arose and fought the well-equipped German soldiers who were their "jailers." Once they knew that they would perish as prisoners if they did nothing, they decided to perish as free individuals. Resistance meant sure death, but it also conferred human dignity and a sense of purpose that gave value to life. They might have concluded that their fate was inevitable: instead they died like free men and women despite the superior force of the Nazis.

There were many individuals who resisted as well. One was Oswald Rufeisen, aged 21, an unlikely resister because of his youth. Born near Oswiecim (German Auschwitz), Rufeisen acquired many languages and became fluent in Russian, Polish, and German. In 1941, with false identity papers, Rufeisen traveled to the village of Mir, where he was employed by the local police as a translator. It was in this position that he was privy to police intelligence. When plans were organized to liquidate the Jewish ghetto in Mir, Rufeisen notified the ghetto of their impending liquidation, allowing some 200 Jews to escape and join the local partisans. He is reputed to have smuggled weapons to the occupants of the ghetto as well.

When Rufeisen was discovered, he was arrested. He escaped, and was sheltered at a Catholic convent. He later joined the Russian partisans. After the war, Rufeisen converted to Christianity and remained in Poland where he became a Catholic priest fighting postwar anti-Semitism. As a consistent rebel against seemingly overwhelming power, Rufeisen shattered many myths.

The Bolshevik Revolution offered itself as the end of history: no more repression, no more czars, no more elites. Even when Joseph Stalin came to power, the myth was perpetuated, supported by the police. In 1936, just prior to the show trials, when the political "opposition" to Stalin would be liquidated, Stalin issued a new constitution. It sounded like a Western constitution. It granted fundamental rights, civil liberties, an independent judiciary, human dignity, and equality. By then many of Stalin's critics had been eliminated, had starved to death, or had been sent to the gulag, writers and intellectuals among them.

Like all tyrants, Stalin raised the flag of Patriotism. Good citizens supported the state. World War II, called the Great Patriotic War in Soviet Russia, helped to marshal support for Stalin. The Cold War that followed divided society further into patriots and dissidents.

What Stalin had learned, perhaps intuitively, was that draconian rule was best realized by dividing the population into rival groups: patriots against dissidents, intellectuals against workers, communists against anti-communists, Russians versus minorities — especially Jews, but also Tartars, Kazakhs, and Chechens; young generation against older generations. Members of the "wrong groups" were stigmatized, isolated, dehumanized.

They became aliens, not citizens (in the Soviet sense).

Stalin conducted a vast experiment substituting himself for the party (and the party for the people). But there were too many of the disappeared. The myth that the future would be better could not be maintained after World War II. After Stalin's death in 1953, within a few years Khrushchev began de-Stalinization. That only made dissidence stronger. The one-party state could not repress what people thought in their living rooms. It could not stop them from reading what dissidents published privately. It could not stop the circulation of contrary ideas, nor could it eliminate the private space in which people discussed alternative futures. It could not silence Alexander Solzhenitsyn, who published his work on the Gulag in the West. It could not silence Andrei Sakharov, a leading Soviet scientist, who stood up for liberal ideas and human freedom. It could not make credible what had long ago ceased to be believable. It could not erect Potemkin villages forever.

What was true of the Soviet Union was also true in the satellite states taken over by the Soviet regime after World War II. Czechoslovakia provided an apt illustration. Václav Havel, in 1978, in the "Power of the Powerless," explained how it was possible for a regime to stay in power whose goals and ideology most people no longer believed. People withdrew into private life, they abandoned public life and acted as if they were loyal to the state, all to maintain the sphere of private life that they could still control. But Havel had a larger point. Myths do not last: when belief in them ceases, they will not survive for long. People are powerless only to the extent that they believe themselves so. People are powerless because they have abandoned public space by implicitly declaring loyalty to the regime, in ways easily recognized by that regime.

Havel posed a question: what would happen when people simply withdrew their implied consent. What would happen when people no longer played the game of implicit loyalty?

What would happen when the myth of irresistible power was shattered?

The answer came in 1989. I happened coincidentally to stumble into history for a few hours in the summer of that year. I had arranged with Janos Kelemen, whom I had met in the US, to exchange ideas about the current status of Hungary and Europe: he was to organize a kind of mini-seminar or conference. Instead, when I arrived, he was organizing a political party. Soon afterwards, he and others were having a state funeral for Imre Nagy, the former President of Hungary, who had been murdered in 1958 for resisting Soviet authorities by withdrawing from the Soviet dominated Warsaw Pact in 1956 (organized by the Soviets in 1955 to oppose NATO). Communism collapsed in Hungary in 1989 because people came to the streets to say they would no longer submit to tyranny. They reclaimed public space. And the eternal heaven of communism disappeared almost overnight.

Coming to Prague the same summer of 1989, everything seemed the same and yet not the same as in Hungary. I had talked to a number of people before coming to Prague, including two correspondents from the *Christian Science Monitor*: there was universal agreement that the revolution in Czechoslovakia was not imminent. It was thought the revolution might never arrive. But that fall, in November, it did arrive. The first demonstrations were led by students. Then other dissidents gathered in the Magic Lantern Theater. The police came, there were beatings, and then more demonstrations on Wenceslas Square in Prague.

There was an irony here. The dissident leaders who spoke for the people, who led the people, who were of the people, did not have much faith in them. Even Václav Havel, later the President of Czechoslovakia, had his doubts. "The line between oppressor and oppressed," he wrote, "runs de facto through each person, for everyone in his or her own way is both a victim and supporter of the system."

Yet the outcome in Czechoslovakia, as in Hungary and

Poland, was that many if not most people wanted to live in freedom, and were prepared to fight for it, willing to risk that what followed would be an improvement and that history could move forward. This sentiment won out. Spontaneously, Czechs shattered the myth that communism was inevitable and eternal, and that Soviet authority would never vanish. The power of the powerless proved superior to tanks.

Chapter 3

Post-Truth: Bear Witness

Truth dies every time we accept fiction as reality. Truth is a victim whenever we succumb to groupthink. And this happens whenever we let others think for us, whenever we accept as reality something that can knowingly be contradicted.

Politics give us examples of untruth every day. Political ads, which are known to be propaganda, become the accepted norm. Politicians attack the Affordable Care Act while they proclaim they are committed to preserving "precondition" coverage that the act insures. A politician claims the right to end birthright citizenship by executive order, although it is protected by the Fourteenth Amendment. Demagogues repetitiously insist that there is no global warming, although virtually the entire scientific community for several decades insists there is. Scientists themselves continue to lose the public debate because conservative politicians claim that we don't know all the facts, although global warming is now incontrovertible. Meanwhile we learn that 60 percent of the global animal population has disappeared since 1970.

The past provides abundant illustrations of the defeat of truth for political purposes. In 1931 the Japanese staged a mock invasion of Japan in order to justify its invasion of China. China has long denied that Tibet was once independent. The British justified their settlement of Australia by insisting that it was nobody's land, effectively erasing 50,000 years of aboriginal history. Democracies have not been immune to the mischaracterization of reality. President Lyndon Johnson famously accused Vietnam of twice attacking US ships in Tonkin Bay in 1964, although it turned out that these were vast distortions of the truth.

Zionists, eager to acquire land for a Jewish state, looked

at Palestine as a land without a people. Simultaneously, they asserted the rights of a Jewish people without a land. In 1969, Golda Meir, then Israeli prime minister, claimed there was no Palestinian people and never had been. As late as 2016, in a speech to the Israeli Knesset, Anat Berko argued there was no such entity as the Palestinian people. Several decades earlier, Margaret Thatcher insisted there was no such thing as society. Donald Trump continues to doubt global warming. On June 25, 2019, France braced for the hottest temperatures ever recorded (45 degrees Centigrade).

The twentieth century has produced many of the greatest falsehoods and the greatest human wreckage. Hitler came to power partially based on his promotion of the fictitious story of the Elders of the Protocols of Zion, a narrative that proclaimed Jews were conspiring to enslave non-Jews and to rule the world. This myth was pervasive in much of the Christian world as well, even before being proclaimed by Hitler. *The London Times* published the story as credible in 1920, only several years later renouncing it as false.

Another myth, known as Blood Libel, in which Jews purportedly sacrifice Christian children to use their blood in Jewish rituals, appeared in Norwich, England in the mid-twelfth century. The accusation of Blood Libel did not die out in medieval Europe. It resurfaced a number of times in late Imperial Russia, in Kishinev and Odessa. As late as 2014, an official of Hamas revived the accusation. He claimed that Jews had never stopped murdering Christian children for their blood.

Germany would only be great, Hitler proclaimed, when it got rid of its Jews. The Nazis murdered more than 6 million Jews, but Germany did not become great. Instead, it lost World War II, millions of Germans lost their lives and Berlin was reduced to rubble.

David Irving has been a consistent denier of the Holocaust. At the least, he has suggested, Auschwitz is a fabrication, a kind of "Disneyland." This is despite the physical remains that prove otherwise: 38,000 pairs of men's shoes, 348,820 men's suits, 836,255 women's garments, and 7 tons of human hair. Then there is the detailed eyewitness testimony from survivors and perpetrators, the blueprints and photographs, the official correspondence and statements by leading Nazis. Challenged in a British court by American historian Deborah Lipstadt, Irving's argument dissolved into smoke.

In July 1995, in Bosnia, the Bosnian Serbs, led by President of the Republika Srpska, Radovan Karadžić, and General Ratko Mladić, murdered at least 7000 Bosnian Muslims at (and near) Srebrenica. Both men denied that the event had ever happened. The 7000, they suggested, had more or less emigrated voluntarily. But the 7000 never reappeared because they had been systematically slaughtered. That was the verdict of the International Tribunal for the Former Yugoslavia (ICTY). The ICTY found both Karadžić and Mladić guilty of genocide.

Adolf Hitler consistently argued that Germany lost World War I because of the Jews. Marshal Erich Ludendorff, one of the leading German generals during World War I, agreed: the Jews stabbed Germany in the back, he proclaimed. Today it is recognized by historians that Ludendorff was one of the primary reasons for Germany's loss during World War I.

Benito Mussolini said that he was chosen by God to rule Italy. He convinced himself, if not too many others, that he was omnipotent or godlike. This image was belied after General George Patton invaded Italy in 1943 and the fascist regime fell. Mussolini proved less than omnipotent. He was killed in April 1945 by Italian partisans.

For centuries, science had to operate in a post-truth environment. When Galileo challenged the then orthodox belief in a geocentric cosmos in the seventeenth century, and suggested in its place an infinite universe, the Catholic Church threatened him with excommunication. When Charles Darwin proposed the idea of human evolution and the possibility that human life (homo sapiens) first appeared on earth hundreds of thousands of years ago, he was met with derision by the Church. It insisted that Creation occurred some 3000 years before the birth of Christ (just as indicated by the Bible).

Post-truth society is incompatible with democracy. Post-truth is post-science. Societies that are post-truth are vulnerable to myth and propaganda. They are susceptible to hatred and exclusion. Post-truth societies are, as suggested by Timothy Snyder, pre-fascist. Once the truth-falsehood border is crossed, once lies become comfortable and unchallenged, once truth and falsehood become relativized (and less distinguishable), the transition to fascism has begun. And it may be irreversible.

Post-truth societies in the past endured for a reason. Some people were deceived, others were fearful. Many expected that tyrants would discredit themselves and fall from the weight of their own deceit. In Weimar Germany too many failed to defend their own constitution and their own institutions. And too many were susceptible to hatred, ethnic divisions, and divisive labels chosen by autocrats.

We should be aware that as soon as science is derided, as soon as expertise is denounced, as soon as facts are relativized, as soon as some people are ostracized because of ethnicity, truth has yielded to post-truth. Democracy has yielded to post-democracy. And the cloud of pre-fascism drowns the sky.

Chapter 4

Nationalism: It Won't Make America or Any Nation Great

Nationalism can be liberal. It happens when populations with national aspirations for their own state are trapped within the borders of empires. The Vietnamese struggled against French colonialism, and then American imperialism in order to obtain their independence in 1975. Cuba suffered from colonial domination by the Spanish and then the American imperium for centuries, until its 1959 revolution. Throughout history, oppressed groups have fought for equality by defending their identities and often proclaiming a state of their own. For Jews, Zionism was a response to anti-Semitism and later the Holocaust. In India, Gandhi used nationalism as a way to fight British colonialism. All of these struggles are liberation movements fought against colonial powers.

Nationalist anti-egalitarian movements are different: they want to preserve privilege. They do not liberate any group. Typically, they diminish the "Other." Immigrants or minorities, Jews or Muslims, for example. In the twentieth century, many (ultra) nationalists have resorted to fascist tactics. They have devalued education and expertise. They have attacked science as a haven for leftists and socialists — as illustrated by Rush Limbaugh and Donald Trump denying climate science. They have castigated the press as a bearer of "fake news." They have replaced the search for truth in an open society with proclamations that serve the interests of ideologues or demagogues: the birther argument that Barack Obama was not born in the United States; the myth that he is a secret Muslim. They have denied the right of parliaments and congresses to establish oversight of the executive. They have attempted to delegitimize universities and experts, and any challenging ideas. The way is then open for fascistic/nationalist leaders to define and describe the reality of their choosing.

For the French fascist, Pierre Drieu la Rochelle, the rebirth of the European man (in 1941) meant rejecting ideas, culture, doctrine: the new European man believed only in direct action. What was important was not ideas, but will. Not complex ideas, but slogans. European man, he said, "believes in acts and carries out these acts in line with a nebulous myth."

What was important was to diminish the individual, to feed his emotional instincts, to eliminate his individuality, to fit him into a mass identity that elevated him over other groups. Hitler understood this intuitively in *Mein Kampf*:

> All propaganda should be popular and should adapt its intellectual level to the receptive ability of the least intellectual of those whom it is desired to address. Thus it must sink its mental elevation deeper in proportion to the numbers of the mass whom it has to grip…The receptive ability of the masses is very limited, and their understanding small; on the other hand, they have a great power of forgetting. This being so, all effective propaganda must be confined to very few points which must be brought out in the form of slogans.

The purpose of propaganda is to instill passion and fear in place of reasoned discourse. Fear is stoked for a reason: to embrace an imagined reality that fits the purpose of the propagandist. It is used to ostracize the "Other." If it is not the Russians, it is the Iranians. If not them, it is the Mexicans. If not them, the African-Americans. If not them, the Jews. Or the opposition party: thus the refrains that have been repeated endlessly by Donald Trump: "Lock her up," "build the wall."

Hannah Arendt, who understood the dangers of ultra-nationalism, especially its German National Socialist iteration, explained how conspiracy theories gained currency in *The Origins of Totalitarianism*:

> Mysteriousness as such became the first criterion for the choice of topics…The effectiveness of this kind of propaganda demonstrates one of the chief characteristics of modern masses. They do not believe in anything visible, in the reality of their own experience; they do not trust their eyes and ears but only their imaginations, which may be caught by anything that is at once universal and consistent in itself. What convinces masses are not facts, and not even invented facts, but only the consistency of the system of which they are presumably part. Repetition…is only important because it convinces them of consistency in time.

Hitler proved that repetition of myths could defeat democracy, equality, public discourse, expertise, universities, and the Open Society. Victor Klemperer, who saw Nazism up close, observed that the sole purpose of Nazi vernacular was "to strip everyone of their individuality, to paralyze them as personalities, to make them into unthinking and docile cattle in a herd driven and hounded in a particular direction, to turn them into atoms in a huge rolling block of stone." The purpose was not just to limit or to oppose another view, but to eliminate its possibility. Not to convince the intellect, but to appeal to the will. What got people to the polls, said Steve Bannon, was pure anger. What the president sells when building the wall is demonization of Mexicans: they become toxic in this mythology. They are criminals, drug lords, and rapists.

The twentieth century saw similar narratives repeatedly. Fascistic politics were invoked as *empires declined*. As this happened, as it did to the Ottoman Empire, the Austro-Hungarian Empire, the German Empire, and latterly to the American Empire, there was a sense of national humiliation. The resurgence of the nationalist narrative was also a chance to reverse history. But that meant finding a villain to explain the apparent victimization. For the Ottoman Turks the villain was the Armenian population. It was also the Slavs. For the Germans it was the Jews. And in America it has become immigrants: Muslims, Mexicans, and increasingly Jews. The resulting narrative in each case of resurgent nationalism has been "remembrance" of a mythic past based on blood or some fictive version of exceptionalism.

Germany likewise suffered a national humiliation during World War I. Unable or unwilling to accept German defeat, much of the Prussian ruling classes awaited an opportunity. It was not long in coming. Adolf Hitler rewrote the past defeat as the work of Jewish plotters. He invoked the Myth of the Protocols of the Elders of Zion: again, it was the Jews that undermined Germany. The Jews that destroyed the mythic German past. The Jews who mixed their alien blood with that of the Aryan Germans. The Jews who robbed Germany of its deserved eternal legacy. The Jews who had no soul. The Jews who could think of nothing other than material desires.

After World War II, Europe had learned its lesson. The future was in union. Free democratic discussion. Not ethnicity, not nationalism, not mythic blood origins. Not demonization. Not exclusion of the Other. Not in the smoking ruins of the past. Not in envy and hatred. Not in invoking ancient hatreds, class conflicts, national greatness. And certainly not in invoking the "end of history."

Or had Europe learned its lesson? Could there be a reconciliation in the absence of 6 million murdered Jews? Could Europe be reborn after the death of a part of itself, "except as a ghost," as Bernard-Henri Lévy said in *Left in Dark Times* The answer was no, the answer was Bosnia. Bosnia was a miniature of Europe. It brought together three nationalities, four if we count those who didn't want to be identified as a separate nationality. It had been enough for Bosnians to be called Yugoslavian, or

European. Bosnia was exactly what Europe had wanted to be.

And then it was destroyed. Yugoslavia imitated the empires, and once again the image of Europe evaporated. Not the end of history but nationalism revived. Bernard-Henri Lévy saw it clearly.

> Europe was there, existing, living, and we let it be blown up by shells, targeted by snipers, shredded by rockets and finished off — to the thunderous applause that followed that of the explosions — by the pitiful Dayton Accords, imposed on President Izetbegović after four years of suffering and which amounted only to a brief pause.

Again history did not end, it returned with the demons of chauvinism, the renewed fixation on origins, the restored memory of motherlands, the bittersweet exclusion of the Other, a new border of blood. In the very bosom of Europe, at the doorsteps of the Holocaust, suddenly a new genocide: suddenly a new rehearsal of nationalism in the former Yugoslavia.

Then the American Empire faltered. There were many challenges: militant Islam, perpetual wars in the Middle East, the reemergence of Russia as a power, the rise of China as an economic and military superpower, the financial meltdown of 2008, endemic social inequality, a global army of migrants and immigrants fleeing war and hunger. And suddenly people felt less protected and more divided, the American Empire became vulnerable. Mortal.

It was a perfect storm, and into the breach rode Donald J. Trump. His timing, though by chance, was impeccable. He arrived amidst the ruins of neoliberalism (the financial meltdown of 8 years earlier) and the ruins of neo-conservatism ("democracy" in the Middle East). He arrived amidst the widespread sentiment (believed falsely) that immigrants posed health threats, that immigrants were costing Americans their jobs. From all this, it was easy to revive the story that immigrants were eroding the American dream. It was the old tale: the decline of empire, the belief in victimization, and the desire to reverse imperial decay and protect those who were formerly privileged. And so White Nationalism emerged in America.

Samuel Huntington was one of the first to notice what he presciently called the long-term demographic and cultural challenges to American national identity. In *Who Are We*, he described the influx of undocumented immigrants and the rapid growth of the Spanish speaking population, "challenging" the traditional hold of white, Anglo-Saxon, Protestant men on the levers of power. He predicted — and warned — that the erosion of power would have a significant backlash. He foresaw exclusivist, mostly white sociopolitical movements that would attempt to reverse history:

> Who would avenge the loss of their social and economic status, stop their loss of jobs to immigrants and foreign countries, stop the perversion of their culture, stop the displacement of their language, stop the erosion or even loss of the historical identity of their country. (Huntington's term is "White Nativism")

The message could not be missed: it was anti-Hispanic, anti-black, and anti-immigrant. It was anti-Semitic and Christian. It was based on white supremacy. It was a theme that Donald Trump would invoke. It is what he tapped into, implicitly, unconsciously. He would Make America Great Again. He would protect the racial purity of the mythic Folk. He would stand sentinel against the Deep State of invisible plotters. He would resurrect American honor against the criminals south of its border. He would protect the sexual honor of women against dark predators (oh the irony). He would build walls to block Mexican drug lords: all this to spur solidarity, a mythic communion, a White Brotherhood.

With Donald Trump, America rediscovered its alter ego: to be great, the president said, demonize the "Other." In this mist of demonization, the true origins of suffering disappeared. Immigrants (imagined enemies) were banned or deported. Jobs were promised to magically reappear (although many never returned). And the real conditions of existence, the real causes of misery became invisible.

Chapter 5

Facts: There are No Alternatives

Like Winston Churchill, George Orwell warned of the great dangers facing the postwar world, even after the defeat of the Nazis. Before Churchill's Iron Curtain speech noting the dangers of the unrestrained power of the (Soviet) state and the long growing shadow across Europe, Orwell wrote, in 1941, "This is the age of the totalitarian state which does not [and] probably cannot allow the individual any freedom whatever." When one thought of totalitarianism, he continued, one reflected immediately on Germany, Italy, and Russia, "but I think one must face the risk that this phenomenon is going to be world-wide." Orwell had sniffed not only the coming Soviet colossus; he had anticipated the all-powerful state "that would forbid people to express certain thoughts and would take an additional step and tell them what to think."

These warnings were to find their expression in Orwell's novel *1984*. The unlikely hero of the book, Winston Smith, is a middle-aged Englishman living in a world in which there is no objective reality: reality is what the all-seeing state says it is. To suppress any opposing or alternative views of reality, there is universal surveillance by the Thought Police using telescreens that transmit and receive simultaneously. It was conceivable, thought Orwell, that the state watched everybody all the time.

Gazing out of his window, Winston sees the building of the Ministry of Truth and the three slogans of the Party: WAR IS PEACE, FREEDOM IS SLAVERY, AND IGNORANCE IS STRENGTH. Orwell describes the other government departments: the Ministry of Peace, that concerns itself with war, the Ministry of Plenty, and the Ministry of Love that is responsible for police functions. The Ministry of Love is the most menacing of all: it has no windows.

Winston may be an unlikely hero, but he knows that reality is something other than what is presented by Big Brother and the super-state. Like Orwell, Winston knows that the most significant act in life is not to speak out or to be published, but to observe accurately the world around him, to trust his own instincts. The most revolutionary act is to collect facts, or to refuse to accept alternative facts. It becomes subversive to insist on this. The most dangerous act is to preserve one's space for independent thought; to reject the Party's insistence that only it can determine what is real and what is not. Thinking is a threat to the state. Denying the right of the Party to decide what is a fact is also an assertion of freedom. For Winston, this meant that life could have meaning. Freedom was thinking independently by refusing conformity. Freedom was observing facts for yourself: "Freedom is the freedom to say that two plus two makes four. If that is granted, all else follows."

A century earlier, John Stuart Mill had already insisted on defining the limits of the state at the point that its power was expanding. Mill saw this as the most vital question of the day, and likely to be even more crucial as the state's power grew. At the very core of liberty, he insisted, stood the domain of the individual, "the inward domain of consciousness...liberty of conscience...liberty of thought and feeling."

Winston's occupation was rewriting history. That is what spurred his rebellion, his insistence that he exists and is human. And therefore he could arrive at independent and critical judgments, although he knew those judgments would not be heard. But uttering truths, if only to himself, somehow carried on humanity. "It was not by making yourself heard but by staying sane that you carried on the human heritage." Elsewhere, Winston says, "If the Party could thrust its hand into the past and say of this or that event, it never happened — that, surely, was more terrifying than mere torture and death." The only way to combat the disappearance of the past, and of those who had been vanished from it, was to rescue the memory of those who had been vaporized or airbrushed from history.

Mind control demands control over how history itself is remembered and memorialized. And it demands also the suppression of that space between the individual and society: there must be no space at all, no private judgments, no independent thoughts. No verifiable facts.

Orwell, like his character, Winston Smith, was something of an anomaly, uttering a truth that many would not want to hear, especially a Left that clung to the defense of the Soviet Union well past the 1940s when Orwell wrote *1984* (it was published in 1949). His message, and his convictions, however, resonated in the Soviet Union where they proved prescient. There, dissidents like Alexander Solzhenitsyn, Andrei Sakharov, and Andrei Amalrick, simply by testifying to the facts they witnessed daily, and which everybody could plainly observe from their windows, or experience in the shadows of the long nights, helped to destroy the Soviet Union only half a decade after the real year 1984.

Orwell had in mind the Soviet Union. But he also feared that totalitarianism — or at least a high level of mind control — was possible anywhere, and everywhere. He was anticipating the surveillance state, the intrusive state that he saw coming inevitably to the West — had he been born later he might have referred to the surveillance corporation. Orwell had the vocabulary that he needed to characterize this dark future, a language that he bequeathed to the modern world: "doublethink," "Newspeak," and in the modern vernacular "GROUPTHINK," a word that Orwell would have found compatible with the emerging vocabulary.

Orwell was thinking of the Soviet colossus, but knowingly or not he was anticipating much of the ugliness of the modern era. Here he is in *1984*:

"Who controls the past", ran the Party slogan, "controls the future: who controls the present controls the past." And yet the past, though of its nature alterable, never had been altered. Whatever was true now was true from everlasting to everlasting. It was quite simple. All that was needed was an unending series of victories over your own memory. "Reality control", they called it: in Newspeak, "doublethink".

Almost 7 decades after the death of Orwell, the modern world has run into the oblique face of doublethink head on. Orwell has provided the definition for it, but it is easy to recognize it in the daily rhetoric of politics. The perversion of language provides a built-in distortion of reality. Orwell linked doublethink to the Party, but we recognize the language everywhere:

DOUBLETHINK...is to use conscious deception while retaining the firmness of purpose that goes with complete honesty. To tell deliberate lies while genuinely believing in them, to forget any fact that has become inconvenient, and then, when it becomes necessary again, to draw it back from oblivion for just so long as it is needed, to deny the existence of objective reality and all the while to take account of the reality which one denies — all this is indispensably necessary. Even in using the word DOUBLETHINK it is necessary to exercise DOUBLETHINK. For by using the word one admits that one is tampering with reality; by a fresh act of DOUBLETHINK one erases this knowledge; and so on indefinitely, with the lie always one leap ahead of the truth.

Orwell's meditations should serve as a warning to the West, and especially to Americans, of how easily power can be abused, and how readily the past can be distorted, or even disappeared in order to serve the "power" of today. Doublethink, in which realities that never occurred are constantly invented and "remembered," are retrieved as needed and as convenient, and instantly excised when inconvenient. Wars, which go on for decades — as they did in *1984* — seem to be a dream, without a clearly defined purpose or enemy: like pasts, which may or may not have happened.

Orwell would have recognized the rise of the intrusive intelligence-gathering state that characterizes both East and West. The US has routinely and consistently killed people in countries with which it was not officially at war, such as Yemen and Pakistan, places where wars drone on, without any visible ends or purposes. Often, people are killed by remote-controlled aircraft. Many of those killed are not identified. They are targeted only because of behavior patterns that the US considers threatening: such as owning a gun, or perhaps having a conversation with a suspected militant.

We recognize the intrusive state, and the powers of propaganda, when Orwell discusses the ease with which the proles can be manipulated,

> To keep them in control was not difficult. A few agents of the Thought Police moved always among them, spreading false rumors and marking down and eliminating the few individuals who were judged capable of becoming dangerous; but no attempt was made to indoctrinate them with the ideology of the Party. It was not desirable that the proles should have strong political feelings. All that was required of them was a primitive patriotism which could be appealed to whenever it was necessary to make them accept longer working-hours or shorter rations.

The key here is that indoctrination is not needed, other narratives are simply denied — and in any case history (fake history) suggests no alternatives. Yet Orwell could hardly foresee how intrusive modern corporations have become, and how invisible that intrusion often is. He could not have anticipated that modern companies like Apple, Google, and Facebook are not about efficiencies: on the contrary they are about the invention of previously inconceivable products. It is these products that companies have used to intrude far deeper into people's lives than the champions of the industrial age, creating an invisible world of massive penetration into the private lives of those dependent on its technologies. The result? Previously, news and print media analyzed corporate structures: today's corporations filter (decide) which "news" reaches their clientele, using logarithms to match ads to the personal tastes of users: tastes that they help to create.

The result is the tyranny of the telescreen where the real world is erased, where fact is often fiction, where fiction is often "fact." The lesson here is clear: be aware of who sits behind the screen. Know who controls the narratives that are spun through the news. Know the source of any and all information. Don't routinely submit to "authorities." Assume responsibility for knowing who and what is authoritative.

Chapter 6

Tyrants: They Don't Speak for the "People"

Authoritarian regimes did not come to power in the interwar period because they were popular: popularity came later, if at all. Yet people who were anything but devotees of fascistic (or communistic) ideals were willing to embrace — or to submit to — authoritarian governments almost overnight. Intellectuals, teachers and professors, legal scholars and attorneys, scientists and ordinary people of all levels embraced ideas that only a fortnight earlier they had loathed or ignored. Some did so out of fear of the regime, others reacted to the scapegoating of minorities, and yet others were loyalists to promote careers or to conform so as not to stand out. Whatever the reason, large numbers of people conformed to the new reality and chose the path of least resistance.

Despite all his utopian proclamations anticipating a golden future, Vladimir Ilyich Lenin's power rested ultimately on the NKVD, a secret state police force that organized the Great Terror throughout the Soviet Union. But the NKVD had ample assistance from local police throughout the country, and both were assisted in their state-sponsored terror by the Soviet bureaucracy. What made the 1930s so brutal in the Soviet Union was the willingness of the police forces, civil servants, and legal professionals to suppress dissidence and commit atrocities at the behest of the regime. Without the active assistance of thousands of these cadres, the Great Terror, and up to 700,000 political murders, might have been averted.

It might be comforting for some Germans to think of the Holocaust as something that the Nazis implemented — without the acquiescence or active assistance of many Germans. Or that the Holocaust was the work of Adolf Hitler, or even the result (exclusively) of the German Secret Police, the SS or *Einsatzgruppen*. But this is to miss the central point that the SS and Hitler could not have been so lethally efficient without the support of hundreds of thousands and even millions of "ordinary" Germans. The inconvenient truth is that millions of Jews were not murdered at Auschwitz or Treblinka or other death camps. They were shot by members of the Wehrmacht, local policemen from Riga to Kiev, and the Order Police who were active in Austria, Poland, Yugoslavia, and the Soviet Union. The Order Police, an auxiliary force composed of middle-aged men — mostly former security force — which included some 100,000 uniformed German policemen by 1939, often acted in concert with the SS, and was responsible for the deaths of up to a million people (mostly Jews) in Nazi-occupied eastern territories.

Altogether, the SS and the Order Police murdered millions of Jews in the field, a sum probably greater than the number murdered in death camps. Members of the auxiliary police were ordinary Germans. They were not specially trained for their tasks, many had not been members of the Nazi party prior to Hitler's accession to power, and many if not most had not been anti-Semites. Yet the vast majority obeyed the order to murder civilians whom they did not know or hate, if for no other reason than they had their orders and did not want to look weak. Others did not want to jeopardize their careers. The few who objected were not punished and were reassigned upon request. But the majority of the Order Police routinely participated in execution orders, annihilated entire populations, and forced local populations into slavery.

The SS and the Order Police could not have murdered millions of Jews without the participation of the Wehrmacht, the civil bureaucracy, the German state apparatus, train engineers, civilian occupation authorities, and tens of thousands of willing (or acquiescent) bystanders. The Holocaust required the participation of much of the German nation in order to efficiently liquidate millions of victims. Many who participated in the destruction of European Jews did not have murderous convictions, nor were they ardent Nazis. But for 4 years they submitted to the wills of those who were relentlessly intent on liquidating entire populations.

It wasn't just military men or policemen who obeyed fascistic regimes. Numerous intellectuals found Adolf Hitler and the Nazis compelling. Carl Schmitt, a German philosopher and legal scholar during the Weimar and Nazi eras, argued that parliamentary, liberal democracy was just a sham, a cover for special interests, anything but the organic "democracy" that he welcomed and that he saw embodied in Hitler. Schmitt was an exponent of the principles of fascism, a movement and ideology that he thought inherently superior to the bloodless, compromised facade of democracy.

Physicist Philipp Lenard, a decade before Hitler came to power, described England as a monster country, and Einstein's work as Jewish physics. Germany's universities were full of professors with views compatible with Nazi ideology, before and after Hitler came to power. Emanuel Hirsch was a famous Protestant theologian who swore allegiance to Adolf Hitler and the National Socialist State in 1933. Johannes Stark, another German Nobel winner in physics, became a Nazi loyalist and willing servant of Hitler. He also denounced Einstein. Werner Heisenberg, yet another brilliant physicist and Nobel winner, (probably) attempted to recruit Niels Bohr, the famous Danish nuclear physicist, for the Nazi efforts to develop a nuclear bomb. At the least, he wanted to get a sense of what Bohr knew about nuclear development in America. He invited Bohr to Berlin, but his invitation was refused.

Perhaps the greatest plumb for Hitler was his appeal to the renowned philosopher Martin Heidegger. It was not apparent to many that Heidegger would become a devotee of Nazism. Hannah Arendt and Hans Jonas, two famous German-Jewish philosophers, were both students of Heidegger prior to the advent of Hitler. Yet, Heidegger regretted, as early as 1929, the "Jewification" of the German spirit. In April 1933, he was elected rector of Freiburg by the university faculty. A month later he joined the Nazi party, a membership he did not relinquish throughout World War II. At Freiburg, he called for a reorganization along the lines of the "Führer Principle," in which university life would merge with the state in serving the Volk. During a speaking tour in the fall of 1934, Heidegger asserted: "Let not doctrines and ideas be your guide. The Führer is Germany's only reality and law." After the war, he never mentioned the Holocaust or the extermination camps in his writings.

Beyond intellectuals who were seduced by Nazism, Hitler enjoyed considerable popular support among "ordinary" Germans. In his diary, *I Will Bear Witness*, Victor Klemperer has described the naïve faith that many Germans retained in Hitler, convinced he would never lie to them. Christopher Browning has written that it was common for Germans to retain the belief that whenever "injustice" appeared it would soon be rectified "if only Hitler knew." Bad things occurred only because the Führer was not aware of them.

It was not just a willingness to serve Hitler, or mere acquiescence, that explains Hitler's rise to power. Like Heidegger, many were devoted to Hitler and agreed, or came to agree, "The Führer was the only reality and Law." Like Heidegger, too many Germans believed that Germany was suffering from the assault of "Jewification" on the institutions of Germany. At first, Hitler was seen as loutish and clownish. Many would continue to see him as both. Yet democracy in Germany was fragile: the financial collapse in 1923, the Depression that began in 1929, erased the security and wealth of millions. Hitler's attacks on individualistic liberalism and its corrosive effects, his anti-Semitic rants against Jewish conspirators, his denial of the legitimacy of political opponents, his willingness to curtail the civil liberties of rivals, his insistence on the close integration of a purer community, his belief that he alone was capable of incarnating Germany's destiny, his conviction that his instincts were superior to abstract and universal reason, found a susceptible audience. Above all, Hitler argued that he was the voice of the "people," the true German *volk*, and he would lead the fight against the corrupt elite and their illegitimate political parties, until Germany — the chosen people — dominated others without restraint from any divine or human law. Many ordinary Germans believed him.

These visions offered a new religion in which an individual could be anchored: a story of redemption and an enemy barring the way to that redemption. In this cosmos, understanding was nothing, faith was everything. Factuality was suspended and replaced by myth. It was not truth that mattered, but blind faith in the Leader. And so Germany was seduced — by choice.

Yet it was possible to push back. German wives married to Jewish men did so, and they were not punished; instead their Jewish husbands were released. Some Order Police refused to submit to the murder of Jews. They were excused. Had the legal professionals, had the civil servants, had the professors and teachers, had the police and military leaders, had the ordinary citizens, refused to be bystanders, had they refused the orders of tyrants, millions of lives could have been spared.

Today's autocrats, from Donald Trump in the US to Vladimir Putin in Russia, have rejected traditional liberal values, including tolerance, compromise, universal rights, and even informed and rational deliberation. They insist there is no objective truth, no rational argument that can steer policy. As in the 1930s, they preach a sense of national victimization, fear of an "assault" on "traditional values," danger from "aliens" abroad, a conviction of imperial entitlement, and a willingness to encourage or to tolerate violence.

Past mistakes need not be repeated. Nothing is inevitable. We have learned the penalty for not insisting on truth telling, and for failing to contradict obvious falsehoods. And this is especially true in Donald Trump's America. We do not need to believe that we are under assault by an invasion of Mexican criminals or Muslim jihadists. We do not need to believe that there is no quid pro quo with the government of Ukraine.

This time around we know better. This time around we can escape the past. A whistleblower within the administration has stepped forward to speak truth to power. (S)he has been joined by foreign policy analysts, career diplomats, military personnel, a member of the National Security Council, and an ambassador to the European Union. Collectively they asserted there was "no doubt," "no ambiguity," that Donald Trump tied military aid to Ukraine in return for an investigation of Trump's political rivals.

It has taken only one person to deny falsehoods and to assert truth. One person's testimony has empowered others to come forward. The difference between the 1930s and today is that professors, civil servants, legal experts, pundits, diplomats, and many "ordinary" Americans have refused to give their consent to what is demonstrably false. Although Donald Trump managed to avoid conviction for attempting to coerce Ukraine to help his efforts for reelection — by withholding military aid — it is still possible to speak truth to power and to be joined by others with a similar conscience.

Chapter 7

Nothing is Inevitable: Everybody Matters

World War II was hardly concluded when myths about the righteous opposition to Hitler began to circulate on both sides of the Atlantic. Yet many European leaders had widely embraced and admired Hitler.

Even before World War II, Italy abandoned democracy in 1922 for fascism, and a decade later, in the 1930s, Germany, Hungary, Romania, and Bulgaria adopted right-wing authoritarianism and tied their destinies to Germany. In 1938, none of the powers in Europe resisted Hitler when Germany annexed Austria. France, Great Britain, and Italy were all prepared to accommodate Hitler as Nazi Germany partitioned Czechoslovakia, beginning in November 1938. Only when Poland was invaded, did Great Britain and France declare war against Germany. By then it was too late to deter Germany. It soon defeated Norway and then occupied the Netherlands, Belgium, and France.

In France, in late May 1940, the British Expeditionary Force was trapped at Dunkirk. Weeks before, on May 10, Winston Churchill, belatedly, became prime minister. At that moment, Britain had no allies; France would soon be on the verge of defeat and Poland was already conquered. Moreover, the Soviet Union and Nazi Germany were allies, the US was years from entering the war in Europe — with no firm commitments, and the Royal Air Force was hardly prepared to counter the German Luftwaffe in the air. Within days of Churchill becoming prime minister, the Soviet Union occupied the Baltic states, Estonia, Latvia, and Lithuania. As for Hitler, he imagined that Churchill would parley for peace. Churchill said that he would not, confounding not only Hitler, but also his own Tory party.

Churchill had consistently said that no matter what

happened in France, he would fight on "for ever and ever and ever." Although he was called to the office of prime minister by King George VI, the king had hoped to give the office to Lord Halifax, the sitting Foreign Minister in the Chamberlain government, which had chosen appeasement in 1938. Moreover, public opinion was not firmly behind Churchill and no doubt would have preferred to avoid a war, especially since so many British politicians had found Hitler rather congenial, or had been unwilling to resist him. Churchill might have thought about a two-front war, by allying with Stalin and the Soviet Union. But that also was not foreseeable in May 1940. And for the time being Stalin was comfortably allied with Nazi Germany.

Churchill's mind was firm from the beginning. On the day that Britain declared war on Germany, his intentions were clear: "It is a war, viewed in its inherent quality, to establish, on impregnable rocks, the rights of the individual, and it is a war to establish and revive the stature of man."

Churchill's long road to prime minister had been full of obstacles. Many, especially among the younger generation, thought that liberal democracy was tired and a relic of the past. Many thought the only way forward was fascism or communism, "dynamic" ideologies that beckoned from Berlin and Moscow toward a mythical future. The famous historian Arnold Toynbee thought that Western Civilization itself might be ending, or at least the Western way of life. Many others, like journalist Louis Fischer, were sympathetic to Stalinism, while Beatrice Webb, a socialist, hailed Soviet Russia as a "future" that should be welcomed in place of the decadent West.

Churchill was not despised by only the younger generation. He was also hated and feared by many of the dignitaries of his own party. He was a constant thorn, opposed to appeasement of Germany and Hitler, a critic of the Tories whom, he claimed, willingly underestimated Hitler.

Today it is largely forgotten that many British Conservatives in the 1930s trusted Hitler (and opposed Churchill). Waldorf Astor, an American-born peer, argued that Americans disliked Germans because of propaganda fomented against Hitler by Jews and communists. Astor believed that some newspapers had turned against Germany because of their Jewish owners. The eminent Harold Nicolson reported overhearing a conversation among three young lords that they would prefer to see Hitler in London than to suffer a socialist administration.

The conservative establishment newspaper, *The Times* of London, co-owned by Lord John J. Astor in the 1930s, strongly supported Hitler during that decade. Even after multiple murders during the Night of the Long Knives, carried out on Hitler's orders in mid-1934 against the leaders of his own militia, *The Times* avowed that Hitler was trying to impose constructive and moderate efforts in order to impose a higher standard of public service on Nazi officials. Even King Edward VIII, who reigned for 11 months in 1936, favored appeasement. When Hitler's troops occupied the Rhineland in March 1936, clearly violating the terms of the Versailles Treaty, King Edward called the German ambassador in London to inform him that he had given then prime minister Stanley Baldwin a piece of his mind (although Baldwin had refrained from resistance because the British people wanted only peace).

Neville Chamberlain, who followed Baldwin and preceded Churchill as prime minister, privately told his sister that Hitler was a man who could be relied upon when he gave his word. And a previous prime minister, David Lloyd George, said much the same thing after meeting Hitler: the latter was a remarkable man. As late as November 1937, Lord Halifax, then Chamberlain's foreign minister, after meeting with Hitler, assured Britain that Hitler had no adventures in mind. A year later Hitler began the dismemberment of Czechoslovakia while Britain welcomed peace "in our time." So determined were British Conservatives to parlay with Hitler, that Thomas Jones, a supporter of Prime

Minister Stanley Baldwin in the mid-1930s, not only had the task of sidelining Churchill, whom he and Baldwin thought dangerous for peace, but outrageously asserted that Hitler might make a good ally for Britain.

Historian Tony Judt put it right when he remembered that until the last year of the 1930s, Churchill was regarded as an "overtalented outsider: too good to be ignored but too unconventional and 'unreliable' to be appointed to the very highest office." Churchill was considered by many Tory politicians too independent, too full of energy, too insistent and unflappable in his views, and disloyal to his own party. As his opponents described him, Churchill was entirely obsolete. So derided was Churchill, that when he spoke in 1934 about his concerns for the future safety of Britain, he was greeted with derision. In February 1935, a prominent Tory, Sir Samuel Hoare, told the editor of the *Manchester Guardian* that virtually no Tory would accept Churchill as leader of the party or as prime minister. And Conservative MP Thomas Moore, in May 1935, heaped scorn on Churchill: not only was the latter well past his prime, he said, but Churchill was entirely deluded in thinking that Germany was rearming for war.

Criticism of Churchill was so strident that he might have thought, by the end of 1936, that his political career was over. Baron Posonby, a leading critic of Churchill, certainly hoped that Churchill's political career was at an end. He praised Churchill's literary and even his political gifts, but he also feared those talents and thought that Churchill ought to be sent to prison should a crisis occur. Lord Maugham recommended more dramatic action: he thought Churchill so dangerous that in a crisis he ought to be shot or hanged.

The House of Commons had much the same opinion of Churchill. It was overwhelmingly behind Chamberlain. George Lansbury was apparently not unique. He had heard all the criticism of Hitler and Mussolini, but he had met both of them and concluded that they were like all other politicians and diplomats. And Harry Raikes, a Conservative MP, thought Chamberlain the greatest European statesman ever for having secured peace in 1938.

Churchill had never been deceived by Hitler. In the House of Commons, in April 1933, about 3 months after Hitler became Chancellor, Churchill argued that Hitler was moving toward a one-party state. By the end of the year, he proclaimed that "the great dominant fact is that Germany is re-arming, has already begun to re-arm." A year later, he was especially worried by the growing strength of German airpower and an immense reserve of armed, well-trained men. The factories in Germany, he added, were working under what amounted to wartime conditions.

The British government remained undaunted, in fact quite the opposite. The predominant view in the halls of power insisted that the path to peace was to avoid an arms race, even to disarm. Peace, said Clement Attlee of Labor, could not be achieved by national defense. He and others advocated for the elimination of national armaments. In this they spoke for the vast majority of the nation.

Even after it was no longer possible to believe in appeasement, even after Germany had invaded and conquered Poland in 1939 and partitioned it with its ally, the Soviet Union, even after Britain had formally declared war against Germany, honoring its alliance with Poland, and even after Chamberlain's policy of appeasement was exposed as defeatist, there was no rush to bring Churchill to the highest office in Britain. Ironically, when George VI sought Lord Halifax for the prime minister's office, Halifax rejected the office because of the existence of Winston Churchill. Halifax, sympathetic to appeasement, knew he would have to include Churchill in Cabinet, where he, Churchill, would be (Halifax thought) unmanageable, insufferable, and unbearable. Halifax rejected the premiership.

It is worth remembering how vulnerable people can be, how

supine and managed they can be in crisis. But it is also worth remembering in times such as ours, that if one man — in this case one extraordinary man — can stand up to a tyrant, then surely the majority of a nation can do the same.

Chapter 8

Neoliberalism: Not So Liberal: We are Dangerously Unequal

Let us begin by asserting a simple truth that is widely known, though never admitted: we could easily erase poverty, hunger, economic slavery, and most if not all wars simply by utilizing the technology that we already have and by redistributing the wealth that we already produce. We have the means, if not the will, and we know the policies, although we renounce them, to make us all more equal. Moreover, we have known all this for at least a century. Yet, we have reached new heights of inequality and unprecedented concentrations of wealth. And as a result, badly flawed democracies that allow super-affluent citizens to use their wealth to acquire ever more power. And a flood of people who feel bypassed by the politics that excludes them and the new technology that makes them increasingly redundant.

In 1917, more than a century ago, amidst World War I and the Russian Revolution, Bernard Russell noticed much the same thing. He offered the following observation in *Political Ideals*:

Few men seem to realize how many of the evils from which we suffer are wholly unnecessary, and that they could be abolished by a united effort within a few years. If a majority in every civilized country so desired, we could, within twenty years, abolish all abject poverty, [reduce] half the illness in the world, [and] the whole [of] economic slavery...It is only because men are apathetic that this is not achieved...With good-will, generosity, intelligence, these things could be brought about.

But it was goodwill, generosity, and intelligence that were

lacking. Russell, however, had a good explanation for why the world was failing to heed his advice:

It is not, as a rule, by means of useful inventions, or of any other action which increases the general wealth of the community, that men amass fortunes; it is much more often by skill in exploiting or circumventing others. Nor is it only among the rich that our present régime promotes a narrowly acquisitive spirit. The constant risk of destitution compels most men to fill a great part of their time and thought with the economic struggle.

What Russell had observed, without quite saying so, was that much of the wealth of the ultra-wealthy of his day was based on inheritance, tax evasion, political influence, or just plain theft. And on explicit policies that failed to challenge monopolies or to preserve competitive markets. It was equally clear, Russell thought, that the "unjust distribution of wealth must be obviously an evil to those who are not prosperous, and they are nine tenths of the population. Nevertheless, it continues unabated."

Free market liberals, who governed after World War I in Britain, France, and the United States, tried to restore, or preserve, the world that Russell wanted to exit. Namely, rampant speculation, no controls over private capital, fiscal austerity, and getting the government out of the way so business could pursue profit.

The result was not what Russell would have liked. Not economic security but insecurity. Not equality but escalating inequality. Not greater freedom and democracy but fascism, and then the Depression. And then Adolf Hitler.

Hitler could have been prevented. He languished until the election of July 1932 — an election in which the Nazis became Germany's largest party. But the Weimar German coalition government gave him a great gift. They practiced economic austerity as commended by Germany's creditors and orthodox financial opinion throughout Europe. As a result, Hitler didn't need to destroy democracy. His predecessors did it for him. Instead of saving German workers from destitution, they drove them into the streets. Surging unemployment, raging inequality — and insecurity — preceded Hitler: and they made him possible. In a word, Hitler came to power because Democracy in Germany had failed. And it had failed because political parties had embraced policies that tolerated social and economic inequality — or failed to reverse them.

The policy reversals starting in the 1970s, and accelerating in the 1980s (especially in the US and UK), resembled the old policies post World War I: low taxes, austerity in fiscal policies, withdrawing states and reduced social protection, allowing markets to be as self-regulating as possible. Milton Friedman provided the nudge this time around. He blamed everything on government. His solution was the free market. Too much unemployment? Get rid of the minimum wage. The solution for poor schools? Privatize education. Health care? Get rid of publicly subsidized programs like Medicare. Retirement? Abolish social security. The income tax? Get rid of it. Unleash corporations to do their free market magic.

Friedman's neoliberalism philosophy became the creed of the major parties in many Western nations. By the 1990s even Labor in the UK and the Democrats in the US had embraced Friedman's ideas: privatization, deregulation, low corporate taxes, austerity became the governing creed. Political choice was flattened. New monopolies emerged. Economic growth slowed. In 2008, it went into reverse. And much of the wealth that was created went to the 1 percent (almost half the national wealth in the US). Almost all of it to the top 10 percent.

For workers throughout much of the West, neoliberalism has meant increased job risk, health risk, education risk, and too often housing risk. Bill Clinton blamed workers. He advised them to get better training, or more education. The jobs were there, he said, but not the trained workers. Much the same has been said in Britain.

The result is a precarious class across much of the Western world: a class that has inherited all the risks of modernity and globalization and enjoyed few of the benefits.

Workers have intuitively understood all of this. Many who had voted for Barack Obama pivoted toward Donald Trump. Polls showed that most of them were not attracted by Trump's policies — only 29 percent said that they were. They saw a vote for Trump as a way to punish the establishment.

Donald Trump promised jobs. He said he would not forget the previously forgotten. He repeated that he would foster employment by building walls. Physical walls against immigrants and migrants. Commercial walls by erecting tariffs. His message was covertly and often overtly racist. He made promises to the most vulnerable. He would lower taxes for them, he would fix health care, and he would build the greatest military ever, establishing himself as chief patriot. Ominously, he hinted that he might not accept the electoral results should he be defeated for the presidency. Later, he declared a national emergency (over the wall) that was rejected even by a number of Republicans in Congress — and is possibly unconstitutional. He challenged Robert Muller's right to investigate him and his White House claiming executive privilege. He has hinted that he might pardon Paul Manafort — indicted on 16 counts that include massive fraud. Trump has suggested, ominously, that he enjoys the support of the police, the military, and even thugs or "enforcers": a naked appeal to violence.

It is worth remembering that we are still a democracy. We can still vote. We are the same people who elected Barack Obama. Many who voted for Trump were rejecting Hillary Clinton. Many who turned the election were in the rust belt. Many were at risk because of the failed policies of neoliberalism and the politicians who endorsed such policies. Lost in this mélange of misery were the triumphal cries of "strong economy," repeated (often) by a sycophantic media. Meanwhile, the forgotten, those bypassed by globalization, those suffering the erosion of jobs and meaningful employment, those on the wrong end of evictions, those facing unaffordable college tuition, those bypassed by a broken health care system, await an alternative to Trump. If and when that happens, we must collectively reduce the social and economic risks to all of us and restore — or draft — economic policies that make us more equal. That is the only way to defeat the Trumps and would-be autocrats of the future.

Chapter 9

France: Revolt against the Elites: Hold Them Accountable

In 1989, in Russia, Poland, Hungary, Czechoslovakia, and the Baltic states, Eastern Europeans were willing to stand up against the colossus, the Soviet Union — after decades of repressive rule.

Poles led the way. They had to act clandestinely sometimes, but they did this by supporting Solidarity, a national union movement led by Lech Walesa. Solidarity meant (eventually) massive public demonstrations. So massive that the government was hardly able to suppress them. Then came free elections and afterwards the electoral victory of Solidarity. When the Russian president, Mikhail Gorbachev, refused to intervene in Poland, it was a signal: the Soviet Union soon collapsed. Communism as an alternative social and economic system vanished.

Since 2008, we have seen another revolution gathering: today it is liberal democracy that is creaking along and that needs serious reform. Spontaneous (mostly) protest has spread to the West, including Britain, France, and Italy. In a massive rebellion against the political establishment, the British voted for Brexit, expressing popular sentiment for exiting the EU — an indication that the political elite had lost its footing. In France, the home of eternal rebellion and social revolution since 1789, the *gilets jaunes* (yellow vests) movement has engulfed the country. The French electorate, once enthused by Emmanuel Macron's promises to solve France's economic and social woes — and by an apparent alternative to right-wing populism — has now become hugely disaffected. The demands of the *gilets jaunes* — who have been dismissed by political elites contemptuously as uneducated, bigoted, and out of touch — have received massive support from much of France, which perceives the elites as out of touch.

That is because Macron has acted regally, like a patrician, while supporting policies that have driven up inequality and eroded living standards. In a word, he has expressed disdain for the ordinary folk. He has done this by eliminating the wealth tax, adding a fuel tax (now deleted) that has penalized the poor, levying a new tax on pensions, and he has done little about a stagnant minimum wage.

The French have many grievances that are not shared in common with Americans. They are frustrated by the inability to control illegal immigration (on a different scale than the US), resentful of EU rules that dictate budget restraints (austerity) and put limits on social welfare spending, and they feel threatened by changing moral codes regarding gender issues — all concerns which have only been addressed by right-wing demagogues who know how to exploit such issues. These are all important, but they need not mean xenophobic recidivism.

There are grievances that the French share with many Americans, including Trump supporters. The French reject unregulated (largely) financial markets, neoliberal austerity, and even abject consumerism. In a word, they refuse to accept or to normalize economic liberalism (neoliberalism), a policy they see (many in the US would agree) as targeting them unfairly and removing the social protection that many of the French crave and deserve. They want modernization of their health care system, and many no doubt would like to see the wealth tax restored. In sum, the French have also rejected their political elites — a conclusion that they share with their American and British counterparts.

Gilets jaunes have not transformed France, but they have served notice without bringing a revolution. They have demonstrated that popular protest not channeled through political parties or unions — the historical circuits of popular voice — can mobilize (without depending on the Internet) a set of beliefs that at least resembles an "ideological" platform on which people can envision a "coherent" and alternative future.

What the *gilets jaunes* have done is to take democracy to the streets. The entire idea of public protest has been to make the invisible, visible: hence the yellow vests worn by the hundreds of thousands participating in a Congress of the Streets.

There has been much to protest. Immediately, upon taking office, Emmanuel Macron abolished the solidarity wealth tax, transferring €41 billion to the wealthiest. He then strengthened the Tax Credit for Solidarity and Employment, a tax credit and exemption program remitting €41 billion annually to French companies, including multinationals. In the 2018 budget bill, Macron established a flat tax that lowered taxation on capital, yielding another €10 billion for the richest in France. He has done little to protect farmers (against globalization) who are increasingly going bankrupt.

What Macron gave to the rich, he took from everybody else. The General Social Contribution income tax paid by pensioners increased. Simultaneously, pensions ceased being indexed to inflation — despite the rising cost of consumer goods. Subsidized contracts were abolished (although this was also a subsidy to employers). And the amount of housing subsidies was lowered by €5 per month for the most disadvantaged.

The *gilets jaunes* are not ignorant provincials. They are not anti-Semites. They are angry citizens who do not need elite educations to teach them the reality they are living. Over the past 2 decades the largest fortunes in France have increased tenfold, while the average purchasing power of French families has fallen by €440 annually since the crisis of 2008. As injustice and inequality have become endemic, Macron has become tagged as president of the rich, or *roi* Macron. He has claimed that tax breaks for the rich were needed to generate investment and to produce jobs. The jobs, however, have not appeared: nor will they. The same claims were made by Macron when he worked for François Hollande. The French simply tired of waiting for both justice and jobs.

What the French have demonstrated is that they can assemble peacefully and have an impact on public policy. They can rally for liberty, equality, and fraternity. They have also shown the world that there is such a thing as populism that is not reactionary, anti-immigrant, and susceptible to autocracy. They have demonstrated the urgency and the feasibility of reclaiming democratic values by voting with their feet.

The *gilets jaunes* do not need the elites to tell them how their interests are best served. They have adopted their own list of People's Directives, and have at least suggested a democratic way forward — bypassing their "betters." The Directives propose a "popular referendum" mechanism that allows laws to be proposed by citizens. Such proposals, with 700,000 signatures, would be sent to the National Assembly, which would finalize a version to be submitted to the electorate. The same initiative would enable the repeal of laws, and approval or rejection of international treaties. Much of this is difficult for the elites to swallow. But there is much to be learned in all democracies: short of real democratic reform, this may be the twilight of the elites. It is time for Americans and citizens of the world to make their respective elites accountable.

Chapter 10

The Road to Freedom? Or Serfdom? Right-Wing Populism

Tyrants (and tyranny) and the populist surge that has sometimes brought them to power in Hungary, Poland, Russia, and the US are a logical, inevitable, and illiberal response to decades of neoliberal (economic) policies. Global market society has destroyed the livelihoods and futures of untold millions with the most tepid responses even from (post) democratic Western nations. The result is a resurgence of tribal nationalism in almost every country of Europe and the US. Emboldened by populist resurgence, tyrants have pushed against constitutional limits, restricted rights and freedoms, stigmatized minorities, and tampered with elections (restricting the right to vote in the US). Independent judiciaries are being reined in (Hungary, Poland, Russia): and even in the US, Donald Trump has tried to intimidate the courts and brought cases to district or regional courts friendly to his arguments, which he might otherwise have lost.

This is not without precedent. The 1930s also saw a resurgence of right-wing populism across Europe, fanned by depression and massive migration of populations, following an earlier failure of global market society.

Friedrich Hayek, the father of modern neoliberalism, and leading defender of (global) market society, did not believe that an unfettered market could lead to autocracy and certainly not to anything like totalitarianism and the complete absence of freedom. In *The Road to Serfdom*, his thesis, shortly, was that Socialism (or any form of collectivism for that matter) inevitably leads to despotism. The Nazis had succeeded because the socialists had already done their work for them, i.e., they had done the intellectual work by weakening the desire for liberty. Hayek meant that by bringing the whole of life under the umbrella of the state, socialism transferred power to an inner ring of bureaucrats, who would stop at nothing to retain that power. Hayek cautioned that Britain was on the same road as Germany had been, led by a left-wing intelligentsia (and Labor Party) that was determined to create a planned society under its absolute power. He forecast doom for Britain, certain that the Labor Party would become something like a dictatorship. Hayek did have a prescription for the future: an unplanned economy, free competition, and a return to an emphasis on liberty rather than equality (security).

Hayek's thesis contained some truth. Collectivism is not inherently democratic, a lesson we have to learn repeatedly. It does give — or can give — (unlimited) power to a tyrannical minority. At the least, it may be impossible to impose limits once that power is secured. And Hayek may have been correct when he argued that intellectuals generally — and in the Britain of his day — were more "totalitarian" minded than the common people.

Yet Hayek's conclusions were bad history and demonstrated little political understanding. The Labor Party did not create a totalitarian state. On the contrary, it established the National Health Service, and maintained much greater social and economic equality (as was its mandate) following a horrendous war. The Labor Party averted a possible revolution: at the least it averted social chaos. It did not create a one-party state, nor did it establish a free market when it came to the health and well-being of the citizens of Britain. Labor, in other words, did what it should have done. It shielded the British public from the kinds of adversities that had to be borne during the war, and granted to that public the prophylactic state that it deserved once the hostilities of war were concluded.

As George Orwell observed in his review of Hayek's *The Road to Serfdom,*

A return to "free" competition means for the great mass of people a tyranny probably worse, because more irresponsible, than that of the State. The trouble with competitions is that somebody wins them. Professor Hayek denies that free capitalism necessarily leads to monopoly, but in practice that is where it has led, and since the vast majority of people would far rather have State regimentation than slumps and unemployment, the drift towards collectivism is bound to continue if popular opinion has any say in the matter.

Getting the past right, resisting the corruption of memory, is a responsibility that we have all inherited. And that is even more true in getting the present "right," including how the present sees the past, and how it uses that past to conjure up images of history for political uses in the present. We have seen that Hayek was sorely mistaken, and that Britain in all probability avoided a catastrophe by not following his advice — advice that was itself mired in misunderstanding the past and confusing Stalin's one-party state with the politics of contemporary (of his time) Britain. The Labor Party was nothing if not entirely distinct from the Bolshevists to the east. If the Labor Party of its time was guilty of anything — if the word guilt may be used — it erred on the side of libertarianism. As the great Laborite Aneurin Bevan — a leader in founding the NHS and in circling the Byzantine pathways where the entrenched medical lobbies resisted any collective solutions (like the NHS) — put it, Labor was that rarest of groups that sought power in order to distribute it to others.

Yet there was a larger point to the wisdom of Labor — a point that is largely forgotten today. The so-called free market does not concern itself with the public good, it does not create institutions that protect the public health, it does not see any of us into a comfortable retirement, nor create clean air, nor impose a carbon tax on polluters. It does not even insist on safe toys for our children, nor does it hold traders with insider knowledge accountable for their insidious cheating. And if markets are left "alone," as Orwell in the past and economists like Joseph Stiglitz in the present have argued, we will inevitably get the kind of social and economic inequality that we don't deserve and that is disrupting civil society on both sides of the Atlantic.

Getting the past right in the present is precisely what we are lacking. The result is that we have forgotten how we got here, and why we have the kind of present (and inequality) that we do have. The policy reversals that occurred in the 1970s, which were intensified in the 1980s, restored classical economic liberalism (now globalized) broadly across Europe and America, forgetting why economic liberalism (neoliberalism) had been curbed to begin with. The policy changes, with the broad support of social democrats, left leaning liberals, and classical conservatives, produced, by 2000, a consensus. Democrats in America, New Labor in Britain, and the Social Democrats in Germany devised the Third Way, shorthand for acceptance of economic liberalism, embracing Wall Street and the City as the surest road to sustained economic growth. The Center-Left, sounding much like the Center-Right, was unable or unwilling to promote credible alternatives to neoliberalism. As wealth became ever more concentrated in fewer hands — in the US the 1 percent controls almost half the tradable wealth, as real competition withered despite free market rhetoric, as monopolies emerged across every sector of the economy, as globalization made tax evasion easier and a favorite device of wealthy elites, as political democracy became less democratic, the various publics, bypassed by the traditional parties, looked to illiberal solutions: especially when those publics were told that they were the problem, that they needed more initiative, or better education, or that they should move to where jobs and opportunities actually existed.

When political elites forgot about ordinary citizens, they

were inviting disapproval not only of themselves, but of the democratic institutions they were failing to defend and that brought them to power. The outcome is the kind of illiberalism that is now enveloping us and the emergence of tyrants more than willing to shelve democracy when it gets in their way. Ordinary citizens have to learn or relearn ways to use the tools of democracy to defend democratic institutions and respective constitutions.

One way is to participate in local politics, after all every national issue is also a local issue, and the converse is just as true. But we must also poll history for some of our answers. We must educate ourselves and know the voices of the past that have faced earlier tyrants and tyrannies, and errant policies. We must know the voices of the present. We must maintain a healthy skepticism. We must reject the inevitability of risk: housing risk, job risk, education risk, retirement risk. Income risk. We must understand how risks of all kinds have been transferred to the public: largely because of tax policies, labor policies, housing policies, education policies, and health care policies. The result is an age of billionaires. An age of inequality. An age of uncertain and temporary employment. An age of social insecurity.

Chapter 11

Progressive Populism: It is Not Extremism

Populism and nationalism are often equated in modern political discourse, but this is a mistake of language as much as of politics. And the confusion can be deliberate. Both Bernie Sanders and Elizabeth Warren are often lumped together as extremists, not just by the likes of Donald Trump, but by virtually the entire health care lobby and even centrist politicians for their advocacy of universal health care, or Medicare-for-all. Sanders has also been accused of extremism because of his rejection of trade agreements as not in the interest of Americans (many of whom voted for Donald Trump). Most notably, Sanders has been tagged as a populist-extremist because his ideas have aroused many of the people who also were attracted to Trump's anti-immigrant messages, and for that matter his pro-gun rhetoric.

Yet many of Sanders' ideas are not only inventions for the future, they actually recall the ideas of the New Deal, ideas that in fact attracted the majority of Americans for decades. Ideas that were the basis of American solidarity and that were understood conventionally to be necessary in the aftermath of World War II.

In a word, Sanders is a realist — not a neo-nationalist trafficking in myths. More than Donald Trump, he is very familiar with the realities of working-class life, and was willing to fight for inclusion of much of the working and middle classes, so recently turned out and excluded from any meaningful social contract.

When Bernie Sanders said that the rules were rigged against the working class, and the middle class, he was echoing the message of Elizabeth Warren (and even Donald Trump). Senator Warren has long railed against bankruptcy laws that favor rich corporations over families. She has demonstrated in detail how student loan contracts can (and often do) leave elderly parents liable for student debts owed to fraudulent private universities. She and Sanders both have publicized how banks have repeatedly written predatory mortgages, often evicting people illegally when they failed to meet re-setting interest rates. One of Sanders' key campaign promises was to make health care universal, affordable, and equitable. When he was criticized for being a utopian idealist, or woefully ignorant, he referred critics to the many countries in Europe, Canada, Japan, and elsewhere, which already had universal health care that was much more affordable and much more equitable (and efficient). It turned out that many of his critics on this issue were the for-profit health insurance companies, the main beneficiaries of health care in the US. When Sanders insisted that the most efficient health care program in the US was Medicare, it turned out that he was right. This was because Medicare is a single-payer, universal health care system (for people over 65) that does not enrich health insurers. And Sanders, like Senator Warren, pointed out that the high cost for drugs in the US was because, unlike countries in Europe, drug companies in the US were deregulated. This obviously was not the result of an efficient market getting prices right. It was because a law was passed by Congress that allowed drug companies to charge whatever they wanted and another law that prevented Medicare from negotiating drug prices for seniors (or getting drugs from Canada).

What both Sanders and Warren have argued is that we have returned to an earlier age of monopoly capitalism, an age when competition has dwindled and a few companies dominate every sector of the economy. We have also returned to an age when anti-trust laws have practically become invisible and are rarely invoked. The inevitable result is the kind of inequality not seen for almost a century. To think that any of this is sustainable, or that it is the result of democracy and democratic institutions, is itself an illusion and unsustainable: not when 1 percent of the population controls almost half the financial wealth.

Which is why both Bernie Sanders and Elizabeth Warren want an economy in which companies again — as they once did in the post-World War II decades — invest in their workers and communities. Senator Warren has already crafted a bill to make this happen (it won't happen organically because financial markets will punish the good intentions of well-meaning executives willing to abandon short-term profit taking). Her proposal would require corporate boards to act in the interests of customers, employees, and communities. This is realistic, in fact it is already happening successfully in Germany, where up to 50 percent of board members of large corporations are elected by employees. Despite today's hypercompetitive global economy, Germany's corporations remain highly profitable and competitive.

Calling Bernie Sanders a radical or extremist, or utopian, should no longer deceive Americans. Citizens should become conversant with the ideas put forward by Sanders and Warren. We should follow the money trail. We should know who will preserve our health care in the future — and who profits from privatized health care today. We should know why drug costs are so high, and who is profiting from them. We should know who really benefits from tax reductions, and who pays for them; and who hides profits in tax havens until they are given a tax holiday by a friendly administration. We should know that the minimum wage has remained stagnant for decades, and that raising it is more likely to create jobs than to eliminate them. We should know that the best way to preserve political democracy is to preserve economic democracy.

Chapter 12

The One-Party State: Don't Let Others Define Truth

Adolf Hitler never got more than 38 percent of the vote in Germany before he came to power. The vast majority of Germans voted for other parties and candidates. Yet once he became the German Chancellor, he quickly transformed Germany into a totalitarian state. He achieved this by invading people's private space, eroding any distance between him (and the state) and them. Once Germans no longer had a private life, the distance between their conscience, their innermost thoughts, and the omniscient state vanished. Tina Rosenberg, in *Haunted Land: Facing Europe's Ghosts After Communism*, has demonstrated how the Stasi, the secret police in East Germany, penetrated into domestic life so completely that spouses had to beware of each other. The Bolsheviks achieved much the same through terror. Everybody was a suspect. Everybody was encouraged to watch each other (for "suspicious" acts or ideas).

Mao's China subjected millions to thought rectification campaigns to transform citizens into obedient, right-thinking subjects. People were encouraged to believe that having individual thoughts, or individual rights, was inherently selfish and anti-social. China used Big Posters of Mao to cultivate the image of Big Brother (authority, safety): opposition was deemed unpatriotic.

The Nazi salute and the image of the Swastika were symbols intended to rally support (solidarity). They became the foundation of a new patriotism. Nazi journals expanded on these images, publishing cartoons depicting Jews as aliens: to be German was to be anti-Semitic. To be Jewish was to be anti-German. Nazis threatened the extermination of Jews, as Hitler did in *Mein Kampf*, because, they said, Jews were conspiring to take over the world.

Hannah Arendt, in *Origins of Totalitarianism*, explained how totalitarian societies work and why they succeed in compromising the human condition: "Totalitarianism has discovered a means of dominating and terrorizing human beings from within. In this sense it eliminates the distance between the rulers and the ruled." Totalitarianism goes beyond incarcerating the body, or simply eliminating it. It captures the mind, and in doing so transforms individual identities into mass identities. Totalitarianism is totally invasive because it subverts the individual will. It erases resistance by enlisting the individual in his or her own subversion. It engineers the permeability of the human being. It insidiously removes the distinction between truth and falsehood, and blurs the line between victim and perpetrator.

In a state of radical evil, it is easy to understand the concerns of Hannah Arendt. Human beings are vulnerable, particularly in eras of transition or disruption such as ours. We do not live today in a state of radical evil, but we do live in a time of shifting borders: moral, sexual, political, social, and geographic. Identities have become fluid. And "truths" have become fluid, accompanied by the politics, rhetoric, and symbols of hatred and division.

Nazis, fascists, and authoritarian regimes in the 1930s knew how to promote the politics of hatred. Keep repeating the rhetoric, keep repeating the hatred until people get used to it. Until it is normalized. Repeat lies. Deny truth. Challenge facts. Encourage alternative facts. Appeal to the heartland by encouraging a sense of national victimhood at the hands of a minority. Suggest a mythic past. Promote a utopian future that excludes "the" Other.

Many of the tactics of the 1930s have reappeared. We should recognize them. Once again we are told about a golden age in the past ("Make America Great Again"). We are propagandized (the birther claim against President Obama). Facts are relativized to create a sense of unreality (fake news). Science is denied (global warming is inconclusive). Anti-intellectualism is promoted (denigration of those with expertise). There are endless appeals to the heartland (minorities are criminals, build the wall, promise jobs in industry, invent domestic and foreign enemies). Reality is relativized (Ukraine, not Russia meddled in the US national elections in 2016).

Today, we are not totalitarian, but we see the corrosion of truth and the invention of myths almost daily. President Trump claims that the Muller Report exonerated him. It didn't. He has flouted his support for the military, although he used his privilege to avoid the draft himself (not just once). And he has tolerated and even trumpeted hatred, by claiming that both sides at the White Nationalist rally in Charlottesville, Virginia in 2017 had decent people, although some (many) of the nationalists were avowed neo-Nazis and anti-Semites. Throughout all of this, the president has criticized the free press as purveyors of fake news. He has encouraged his followers to berate political opponents ("lock her up"). He has attempted to bypass Congress by unilaterally transferring military funds to build the wall at the Mexican-US border. And he has used the social media to spin narratives that manipulate public opinion and that blur the distinction between truth and falsehood.

There are ways to combat falsehood. Know who the experts are. Rely on the free press. Listen to religious leaders who have a conscience. Know where to find facts and valid data. Attend public lectures. Rely on what you see with your own eyes. Don't be distracted by the Internet. Read well-informed books written by reliable authors.

The following books helped inform this essay: Hannah Arendt, *The Origins of Totalitarianism* and *The Human Condition*; Czeslaw Milosz, *The Captive Mind*; George Orwell, *1984*; Bertrand Russell, *Philosophy and Politics*; Bernard-Henri Lévy, *Left in Dark*

Times; Colin Crouch, *Post-Democracy*; Timothy Snyder, *The Road to Unfreedom* and *On Tyranny*; Marci Shore, *The Taste of Ashes*; Jason Stanley, *How Fascism Works*; Peter Pomerantsev, *Nothing is True and Everything is Possible*; David Graeber, *The Democracy Project*; and Steven Levitsky and Daniel Ziblatt, *How Democracies Die*.

Chapter 13

Language Matters: Use It Carefully

The absence of civility in politics is the result of the weaponizing (and debasing) of language. In a country that values freedom of speech, which is inscribed in the First Amendment in the American Constitution, that speech is abused with impunity. The Internet makes this worse because people can use abusive language anonymously, without worry they will incriminate themselves, or even be identified.

Political campaigns may not be anonymous, but they do take advantage of the protection of freedom of speech to protect untruths. The result is massive deception, deliberate falsehoods and (often) the use of language to promote fear.

Fascists knew all this very well. Their agendas called for "enemies": find them and destroy them. Or prevent them from entering the country. Stigmatize the way they look, their beliefs. Criminalize them, deprive them of their humanity. For the Nazis this meant characterizing Jews as aliens, conspirators against the German nation. For Turks in 1915, during World War I, it was Armenians who were "conspiring" against the Turks (by hypothetically supporting Russia during the war). Serbs, in 1992, called (Bosnian) Muslims the oppressors of the Serbs throughout history just as Serbs were on the eve of committing genocide against Bosnian Muslims at Srebrenica.

Religion is a faith. But for centuries it has been abused and used as a crusade against other faiths. As early as the fourth century Christians railed against Jews, mostly because Jews did not accept Jesus as Son of God. Later, to be Jewish was racialized. Martin Luther said Jews could not convert because of their "blood." He used the language of hate. Jews who refused to recognize the Lord in Jesus, he said, did not deserve to live.

Even philosophers thought highly humanitarian, Johann Fichte, for example, argued that Jewish heads had wrongful ideas: their heads should be lopped off. Immanuel Kant uttered many of the same ideas, though he preached a brotherhood of humanity. He depicted Jews as "a nation of cheaters," they were "a group that has followed not the path of transcendental freedom but that of enslavement to the material world."

Artful lying was not invented by modern political parties. Using language for political advantage and power has been practiced throughout history. Machiavelli argued that the effective prince had to practice deception to acquire power. The prince had to appear to be good, but should be capable of intrigue and deception. Propaganda (language distortion) became almost a "science" when Hitler used it to acquire office. Joseph Goebbels knew well the skills of false representation. The secret was endless repetition, regardless of what was right or wrong. The same idea appears in George Orwell's *1984*: right is wrong and wrong is right. The most effective way to contaminate the world, and the ideas representing it, is to reinvent language. First invent an "enemy," and then invent a paradise in a post-historical world in which the enemy has been vanquished. The Nazi Aryan paradise of pure-blooded Germany would appear with the disappearance of Jews and other minorities. The proletarian paradise would emerge after the repression of the bourgeoisie. The greatness of America would be reincarnated after the expulsion of Mexicans and Muslims.

In the current political cycle, hate and divisive language reappear. Language is transformed. Political opponents become apocalyptic enemies. Democracy becomes its opposite: an obstacle to "truth." Civility turns into rancor. The search for consensus is transformed into the fight for advantage. Collaboration gives way to hardening of ideologies. The middle evaporates into extremes. The common good is replaced by individual privilege (which is then called the same as the common good).

Labels replace individuals. Ultra Conservatives warn against the "radical socialist" agenda of the Left: higher taxes, big government, big spending. They rail against socialistic single-payer health care that will cost trillions (although a number of countries with universal health care systems are anything but socialist and all of them are less costly and more efficient than American health care). They defend the freedom of speech to help deny that freedom to those they disagree with.

This is the politics of fear becoming the politics of hatred. What is missing in all of this is democracy: liberal and social democracy. Civility, truth. As inflammatory rhetoric rises, as the aisle between political parties widens, the people's business is suspended. Government is closed, and a threat is made that it might not reopen for months or years. A president gleefully takes credit for the closing. Talk shows scrutinize his intentions, politics drones on. Political discourse becomes centered on personalities, in particular the personality of the president. It is not health care that matters, or progressive taxes, or the future of work, or the survival of the planet, but the border wall with Mexico. The will of the people is not discussed. Instead a president insists that he wants the wall and that is what the people want (although the vast majority deny this).

As in a number of autocracies, America now lives in an era in which language has became amorphous. The Democrats are hardly socialists (even those who welcome the title), yet that is the label routinely attached to them by political opponents. This is despite the fact that the Democrats are much less liberal (and social democratic) than they used to be. Republicans are not full-fledged fascists, although some are at the border. Too many have supported Trump's irresponsible rhetoric of hatred. Too many have become opportunists, going wherever the money (power) is. Too many have been willing to normalize and to relativize expressions of contempt for minorities.

The Trump administration, meanwhile, has severed rhetoric

from reality. Reality is now defined by PR. Lower taxes on the rich is called a tax break for all of us. Abolishing the Affordable Care Act (which has provided health care for many millions) is labeled a benefit for everybody: although no replacement is even mentioned. Meanwhile, allies abroad are accused of using the US as suckers.

Why do so many people accept inflammatory language as valid? Because it always has "some" truth. And because falsehoods are insisted upon with regularity. We know how difficult it is to doubt when we ourselves are unsure and we are confronted by persistence in the form of demagogues. They are always certain, mainly because they are not concerned with truth. They are the "truth," or at least they declare the right to define it.

Hannah Arendt, in *Essays in Understanding,* says that "fascists are not happy with lies, they want to transform them into reality." If a lie is false because it does not conform to reality, then change reality until it corresponds to the lie. If the vast majority of Americans do not want a wall between Mexico and the US, remind them that criminals cross borders without a wall. Then declare that many who show up at the wall are criminals. Then say that most Americans wanted the wall to begin with for protection against Mexican and Central American criminals. First say there is a fire: when others can't see it, don't forget to light it.

We know that many nation-states in the past and present have relied on myths in order to preserve power. It is easier to rely on false rhetoric that people will believe, than to use brutal suppression. When people give their consent to a lie, they are accepting the lie as truth, or as not worth rebelling against.

Modern autocrats like Vladimir Putin have resorted to violence if necessary. But, even more effectively, Putin has preserved the shell of democracy without the substance (so-called sovereign democracy). There are still "political parties," there is still a "free press," there is still "freedom of speech," there is still an "independent judiciary." All this in theory (rhetoric), as long as Putin and the state he presides over are unchallenged. Is anybody deceived by all these fictions or mischaracterizations? Probably not, but Putin remains immensely popular, partially by creating enemies abroad, and reconstructing — however minimally — the ancient empire by annexing the Crimea. And by using social media, tampering with elections abroad as in the US, he has recreated the myth of Russian invincibility. Fiction, it seems, in Russia as in the US, can be greater than reality. Which is why we should be able to identify it when we "see" it.

Chapter 14

Beware Technology: It Is Not Neutral

Adolf Hitler intuitively understood how he could use the new technologies of his era to gain access to power. He used radio to give him a mass listening audience, reaching all German households that owned a radio. He used the microphone to blast his voice into the corners of large auditoriums, heightening the drama of mass rallies. He used aviation to attend numerous rallies in a single day, suggesting a sense of omnipresence throughout Germany. He used the new techniques of cinema, employing documentary filmmaker Leni Riefensthal, in *Triumph of the Will*, to film him descending from the sky into Nuremberg — like a deity — to attend the annual Nazi party rally.

Overnight, radio helped increase listening audiences from the hundreds or thousands to the hundreds of thousands, even millions. These audiences were mostly passive: radio was not interactive. One could listen and react, but not interact.

Then came television. Images were now joined to text. Audiences grew, almost everybody in the US had a television in their living room within a generation. The impact grew as well. Images conveyed hidden messages. Ads could compound those messages. Yet the messengers remained invisible. And the temptations were irresistible.

It was, said Neil Postman in *Amusing Ourselves to Death* and *Technopoly*, the Age of Technopoly. The entertainment media overwhelmed us with endless images. It stimulated our desires. It expanded our pleasures. It reassured our futures. It claimed to enlighten us. And it provided experts who told us what and how to think. In a word, it subliminally suggested that the entire world was only a switch away and all we had to do was claim it.

Postman, a technological determinist, argued that the

entertainment media, and the delivery systems of that media, distorted the way that we thought. It diminished our ability and willingness to engage with each other as citizens. It transformed us from citizens into consumers. It invisibly supplied our subconscious with a reality as portrayed on the screen. Instead of critical thinking, millions of us consumed the reality that was presented. Television, said Postman, became a meta-medium. It contained and altered many (or all) previous media forms. By 1985, if not earlier, it became "an instrument that directs not only our image of the world, but our knowledge of ways of knowing as well."

Television became a myth, said Roland Barthes. It was absorbed into everyday life so completely that it became unremarkable and invisible. It was unnoticed and eternal, as if it had always been there. Like all myths, television was a way of understanding the world that was not problematic, a way that we were not conscious of because it was deeply embedded in our consciousness. Once a novelty, television became conventional. We could no longer remember life without it. It was so deeply embedded in us that we could not examine its impact on the way we thought and understood.

The problem with television, Postman insisted, was that it eliminated alternatives to itself. "It does not make them illegal. It does not make them immoral. It does not even make them unpopular. It makes them invisible and therefore irrelevant." When television reached its apex in 1985, its domination over minds and lives was complete. And yet this was hardly understood, and rarely acknowledged.

A generation later, Siva Vaidhyanathan, Postman's student, and Douglas Rushkoff would apply Postman's logic to the social media, especially Facebook. "So while we still read books, attend lectures, argue from adjacent bar stools," said Vaidhyanathan in *Anti-Social Media*, "all of those exercises disappear from what matters…If it didn't happen on Facebook [or other social media], it didn't happen."

Facebook became the new television. No later than 2016, it reached its apex. Like television, Facebook's domination on our screens, in our lives, and over our thinking had many dangerous aspects that remained invisible to most if not all of us. False and misleading information was readily amplified on Facebook. Facebook was the perfect vehicle for spreading information pollution. Fact and fiction were constantly blurred by flurries of "fake news" prior to the 2016 elections. The *Facebook News Feed* presented images that were visually indistinguishable from YouTube to the *Washington Post* to Target store advertisements. Commercials and serious investigative content were presented in the same format. In the lead up to and the aftermath of the 2016 election, Siva Vaidhyanathan has reminded us, "absurd lies about the major candidates echoed around Facebook. And that's largely because Facebook has none of the cues that ordinarily allow us to identify and assess the source of a story." Since then Mark Zuckerberg has expanded on his views: absurd lies are fine with him because they are covered by freedom of speech. Lies are protected by the First Amendment.

Facebook has become the supreme arbiter, the manager of what we see and how we understand what we see. Facebook, adds Rushkoff, "does things on our behalf when we are not even there. It actively misrepresents us to our friends." It conceals and denies its role in political campaigns, which it treats as so many advertising and marketing opportunities. We get so used to communicating through Facebook, we are not aware of how it has changed our vision or our understanding of the world. Welcome to the world of Technopoly.

Facebook granted a major advantage to the Trump campaign in 2016. It was an active partner in shaping the electorate. It was the circuit through which everything traveled: fundraising, message shaping and delivery, recruitment of volunteers, merchandize vending and even voter suppression. Facebook was a political consultant (ad placement). It was a distribution outlet. It was a collaborator of the Trump staff.

As the Trump campaign discovered, it was easy to place ads on Facebook. Facebook did not insist on accountability. It was indifferent to transparency. The Russians discovered the same thing: credibility didn't matter. Truth didn't matter, not to Facebook. Political ads didn't have to be accountable; Facebook made them exempt. And they didn't have to be transparent. As Alex Stamos, former head of security at Facebook, reported:

> We have found approximately $100,000 in ad spending from June of 2015 to May of 2017— associated with roughly 3,000 ads — that was connected to about 470 inauthentic accounts and Pages in violation of our policies. Our analysis suggests these accounts and Pages were affiliated with one another and likely operated out of Russia.

Facebook — and other social media — has prospered from the erosion and hollowing of democratic practices and norms. Facebook is a business, a commercial enterprise that thrives by bypassing democratic norms of accountability and transparency. Its ads, which are not scrutinized, are intended for niches. They are not viewed by anyone outside that niche. The ads are ephemeral. They can promote falsehood or misinformation. Since they are ads that target a niche, they remain largely invisible. Nobody, says Siva Vaidhyanathan:

> could respond to or even question the claims made in such ads. No one could criticize a group or campaign for its practices or run a response ad...An ad could falsely accuse a candidate of the worst malfeasance forty-eight hours before election day and the victim would have no way of knowing it even happened. Ads could stoke ethnic or gender hatred and no one could prepare or respond before serious harm occurs...

Anyone can deploy Facebook ads. They are affordable and easy.

And there are 2 billion Facebook users, all potential victims of a global assault on democracy. That assault has begun. Armies of virtually invisible "bots" move propaganda through Facebook and Twitter. Their objective is to undermine trust in democracy. Their tactic is disinformation. Their hope is to sow divisions and to undermine trust. They have been active across continents in countries as diverse as the Philippines and India, France, the UK, and the US.

Facebook sees itself as a civil servant, as a prop for democracy by bringing people together in a virtual world, a virtual global community. But it is a cornerstone of Technopoly. It remains opaque to itself. It is the ideal vehicle for authoritarians who have more resources than their opponents. Autocrats organize counter-movements against citizen protests. They frame the public debate because they have superior resources and technical expertise. They plant "friends" to corrupt or mislead virtual discussions. They replace public deliberation with unverifiable and misleading babble. They can even steer protest as a way for people to ventilate, in place of actual public protests. They doctor images, take text out of context, compromise and divert reformists and activists. They create cyber troop teams to create fake accounts, or "bots," to interact with and mimic human actors.

Bots have been deployed by government actors in Argentina, Mexico, the Philippines, Russia, Saudi Arabia, and Turkey. Bots flood social media networks with spam and fake news, amplify marginal voices, and inflate the number of likes, shares, and retweets to create a false sense of popularity or relevance. Facebook — and other social media — is their vehicle.

Mark Zuckerberg somehow missed all of that. By November 2017, Facebook had to face reality. The Russians had purchased advertisements on Facebook and Instagram that were targeted to reach a minimum of 126 million Americans. After this revelation, Zuckerberg promised that he and Facebook would do better. But Facebook, as before, is not the platform to find sober and measured accounts of the world.

The Internet is hardly totalitarian, but neither is it neutral. And as we learn, it can be used to manipulate and distort. It robs us of our agency (Hannah Arendt presciently noted the eradication of subjectivity as another consequence of totalitarianism). It is anything but value free. Companies like Facebook, which presume their own innocence, routinely sell the data that they accumulate by watching us. If this were only about selling vacuum cleaners or smart phones, then there would not be anything of concern. But when platforms can be used by foreign governments to promote their interests, intervening in American elections or elections elsewhere, for the purpose of distorting democracy, or weakening opponents, then it becomes the responsibility of users (as consumers and citizens) to become alert as never before. The result is an unprecedented crisis of democracy that we are hardly conscious of — although Donald Trump has, unintentionally, helped to alert us.

What Facebook is doing is converting us, and our wills, into algorithms. We are studied, converted into digital data, and sold to the actual customers, who then can invade our digital space at will. We no longer define ourselves. The corporation is doing that for us, with our active assistance. To the customer, and to Facebook, the seller, we are just so many social graphs, all based on information we willingly give away. The result is that privacy is disappearing and total surveillance — the tool of authoritarians — is already here. If we are our data, we can be watched and manipulated by the buyers of that data.

In 1964, Marshall McLuhan (presciently) published *Understanding Media*, an analysis of the effects of electronic technology on the human brain and human understanding. The argument was succinct and largely unheeded: "The medium is the message." McLuhan was referring to the transformative power of the new electronic technologies. "The electronic technology is within the gates and we are numb, deaf, blind and mute about that power."

The vast majority of users of the Internet conclude that what is important is the content, not how the content is received or delivered. Yet that would be to miss McLuhan's argument. The World Wide Web of today is a total linkage of all information, and it is accessible as never before. The ease and availability of searching makes it possible to jump between digital documents instantaneously. But in this kind of searching, attachment to any one text becomes more tenuous and provisional. Searches lead to fragmentation of works, made even more segmented by search engines that are programmed to offer snippets of information — accompanied often by ubiquitous commercials. "We don't see the forest when we search the web," says Nicholas Carr in *The Shadows*. "We don't even see the trees. We see twigs and leaves."

The coincidence of the technological crises noted above with climate change, political crises from America to Brexit, the Euro (and EU) crisis, masses of migrants fleeing war and the collapse of economies, means that citizens must fight more than ever to avoid using the Internet only as a distraction. The more we see only twigs and leaves, the less likely we are to see that the medium itself is the forest. And the more likely that we will be an object of consumption, susceptible also to political demagoguery.

It is crucial for people to start or to continue meeting each other in person, whether in public spaces or in private homes, whether at political rallies for like-minded candidates, or at our own political rallies. It is time to promote political candidates who will fight for Net Neutrality, who will regulate or break-up the big tech companies that have preferred profit before democracy, self-interest before the common good, their freedom as opposed to yours. If we have learned anything, it is that authority should never be given a free pass. Otherwise, we will be watched and converted into products, not the free actors that we suppose ourselves to be.

Chapter 15

Nothing Is True, Everything is Possible: To Be and Not To Be

"Nothing is True, Everything is Possible": Thus begins Peter Pomerantsev's plunge into the realities and fictions of post-Soviet life. In a word, in post-Soviet Union Russia there is little to distinguish between fact and fiction. Everything from elections, to public dialog, to wealth and who owns it is so oblique that it is part of a giant (sur)reality show. A reality that has melted and been magically transfigured according to the political convenience of those who need myths to buttress their power.

This might not matter to Americans, after all post-Soviet realities seem far away, marooned in their own cocoon, unlikely to impose falsehoods on a distant US. Americans prefer an insular reality of their own. They don't quite have to worry about spillovers of refugees from the Middle East — not at all before 2001 — since the exodus has largely been to Europe, the suburbs of Paris or Brussels, the conurban conglomerates of Scandinavia or the recesses of London.

Americans don't cross borders as often as Europeans, or trade currencies, or even experience terrorist acts — despite the horrors of 2001, as often as their European counterparts. At least they didn't. Which is why the conjunction of Russian intrusion into US electoral politics, the emergence of China as a trade rival and as a military power (and as impending technological leader), the birth (and failure) of liberation movements in the Arab world, the technological revolution and growing joblessness — and the erosion of manufacturing jobs — have challenged the once stable world of the West and its faded but (once) widespread colonization of much of the rest of the world. The result is a series of unprecedented disruptions to the liberal-democratic order established post World War II.

That order begins to dissolve when there is open hostility to verifiable facts and shameless repetition of myths put in their place. Or slogans are used that hint at criminality, leading to chants such as "lock her up" in reference to Hillary Clinton. And as Timothy Snyder has reminded us, there is the element of magical thinking, or empty promises, a rhetoric which allows us to renounce our personal wills and responsibilities so we can rely on a quasi messianic figure to eliminate our national deficits, insure our individual health, cut the national debt, lower taxes, and build up the military. That these promises contradict each other doesn't matter to a mythmaker. When confronted with the distortions, lies, and false accusations, the reply is always the same: anything that contradicts the president is fake news.

Magical thinking has characterized all authoritarian regimes. It thrives when people start believing that they no longer matter, or that they are vulnerable. When they think that democracies have abandoned them, when they find themselves marginalized socially or economically, or politically, and when they no longer feel in control of their lives and their futures. When life becomes too difficult, when a new world order emerges without a name, when all that is solid melts into air (Karl Marx), life becomes unbearable, and amorphous. It is then, says Fyodor Dostoevsky, in *Notes from Underground*, that the tyrant emerges fully into life, only not as tyrant but as (pseudo) messiah:

Why, we have come almost to looking upon real life as an effort, almost as hard work, and we are all privately agreed that it is better in books. And why do we fuss and fume sometimes? Why are we perverse and ask for something else? We don't know what ourselves. It would be the worse for us if our petulant prayers were answered. Come, try, give any one of us, for instance, a little more independence, untie our hands, widen the spheres of our activity, relax the control and we...yes, I assure you...we should be begging to be under control again at once.

We reenter a brave new world in which Americanization is replaced by Russification, in which facts are turned into fiction, and fiction becomes reality. Where "nothing is true and everything is possible." Where nothing seems possible but everything is true. Where everything is temporary and eternal at the same time. And words mean everything and their opposite. We enter the world of Donald Trump. But we enter also the world of Vladimir Putin — and his longtime publicist Vladimir Surkov — who helps us define magical thinking, and gives us hope in the new faith that he defines. The world doesn't need democracy any more, having touched or dreamed of the Golden Ring.

Surkov, the political technologist, Wizard of Oz, special assistant to Vladimir Putin, mastermind who sits behind a desk with a phone bank of all the "independent party leaders," their names spelled out on the phones, calling, directing them at all moments. This is the new authoritarianism: it doesn't need to oppress the opposition. It simply climbs inside their heads, inside all ideologies and movements, until all ideas, hopes, plans are rendered harmless and absurd. For democrats, Surkov funds civic forums and human rights NGOs, for nationalists he accuses NGOs of being tools of the West. For artists, he sponsors art festivals for provocative modern creators in Moscow. Then he counters by supporting Orthodox fundamentalists, dressed in black and carrying crosses, who attack modern art exhibitions. Surkov, who understands the message of the Kremlin well. Surkov, the mastermind and messenger. Surkov, who owns all forms of political discourse. Surkov, the political chameleon.

This Moscow, says Peter Pomerantsev, "can feel like an oligarchy in the morning and a democracy in the afternoon, a monarchy for dinner and a totalitarian state by bedtime." That is what living in a surreal world is like, nothing is real, everything is possible. The opposition can feel like it is an opposition, liberals can feel that they still have a free voice. And the Kremlin can point to their irrelevance.

Surkov claims that the president (Putin) was sent by God. He, Putin, has a conscience, or at least he knows there is such a thing as a conscience (and truth). But the point, to use the words of Timothy Snyder again, is to invoke "implausible deniability." God (as Putin) does evil things, but, as Surkov writes in lyrics for a rock group, "He is always ahead of us in scarlet silk on a pale horse. We follow him, up to our knees in mud and our necks in guilt. Along our road burn houses and bridges. I will be like you. You will be like him. We will be like everyone."

Surkov was the alleged (actual) author of a novel, *Almost Zero*, published in 2008 and based on his own experiences (including as personal assistant to Putin). Even in the Forward, which Surkov acknowledges as his, he contradicts himself and reverts to the shadowy world in which he lives. Simultaneously, he calls the author of the novel a "Hamlet obsessed hack," but then the same volume becomes "the best book that I have ever read." In the world of *Almost Zero*, everyone and everything is for sale, a transparent reference to contemporary Russia. Publishing houses hire gangs, which then shoot each other over the rights to Nabokov and Pushkin. Texts are bought from impoverished underground writers, whose works are then sold to rich bureaucrats and gangsters who publish them under their own names.

Everything is a lie in the world of *Almost Zero*. Freedom is acknowledging that the only truth is that everything is a lie. There is no reality. There are constant mutations: Soviet stagnation followed by *perestroika*, collapse of the Soviet Union, liberal euphoria, economic disaster, oligarchy, and the mafia state. It is impossible to believe in anything except cynicism. Or laughter, eternal laughter.

This was the only road to survival for many in the post-Soviet reality or surreality, and Surkov took it. He switched ideologies and masters through every iteration, reflecting all of this in *Almost Zero*. After all, everything was an illusion and nothing was true. The protagonist of *Almost Zero*, Egor, was beyond good and evil. The world was a blinding abyss of pathless words, of free-floating beings projecting different realities spinning like a kaleidoscope. To master this world, post-Soviet leaders had to be supermen. They had to be stronger, more clear-headed and more flexible than any leaders who had come before them. In this world, human rights and freedom are blunders, misnomers, intrusions from a nether-world, the West, where they exist only as illusions. The only reality is PR, or representation of the world as it doesn't actually exist.

The West was, therefore, no different from post-Soviet reality: all that really mattered was not to have convictions, but to shape them for others. And this was critical in an elastic world where convictions could only be illusions and truth could only be the absence of truth.

Thus, we enter the world of Surkov. Survival depends on dissimulation. Surkov masters this well. His world is not bound by reality, or facts. He determines the facts and ultimately the realities. In the same breath he can be a liberal modernizer and a Russian nationalist: a believer in "managed democracy" and "conservative modernization." Surkov is postmodern: no more grand narratives, no more possibility of truth, only "simulacrum" and "simulacra." But then, and at once, Surkov says that he despises relativism and embraces conservatism. In a world of total illusion, there are no contradictions, only assertions. Again, we are beyond good and evil.

Once upon a time, Surkov continues, the West used parliaments and democratic politics, investment banks and free market economics, and expressionist art or cool culture, to defeat the Politburo, planned economics, and social realism. At last we confront the genius of Surkov, which is also the mirror of post-Soviet contemporary thinking, a pure reflection of the world according to Putin and those who surround him. This is the anti-Western revolution, combining liberalism and anti-liberalism, modernization and tradition, free market economics and planned economies. Absent are clear associations like democratic politics, or free market economies. We now face Surkov's inner world, and that of his post-Soviet associates. Surkov's genius is in his liquid language. He merges authoritarianism and modern art, he validates tyranny by using the language of rights and representation, he edits democratic capitalism until it means its opposite.

This sounds strange to Western ears. But it does strike a chord. Haven't we heard some of this before in America, and in Britain and in much of the West? Hasn't the vernacular of Surkov invaded our own discourses, has it not intruded into the sanctity of our own personal thought, our fleeting consciousness? And just as insidiously, the converse. Didn't the West promise Soviet citizens, in the aftermath of communism, that the market economy and democracy would bring them, well, much of what the West already had: democratic capitalism, freedom, and prosperity? Do we suspect a strange solidarity here? And if so, what to do about it?

There is one reality in Russia, the reality of kleptocracy. So Surkov's responsibility, which is echoed in *Almost Zero*, is to make facticity disappear. To induce a dream like state of innocence. And from his lofty perch as director of publicity of *First Kanal*, Russia's premiere state-owned television station, he could, through adept use of PR, promote the idea that the only truth is the absence of truth. The idea is already there in *Almost Zero*. Through the portal of Christianity, Surkov has a nun cite First Corinthians 13:13: "Uncertainty gives hope. Faith. Love." But Surkov inverts the hope of uncertainty in Scripture. Keep people uncertain by provoking crises, and in this way manage people's emotions. The implication is clear: facts are uncertain, or rather they mean whatever Surkov and the political class says they are. Power is real, and it can define reality. It can choose the facts that it wants: and then publicize them through *First Kanal*. And later, when convenient, it can globalize its view of the cosmos: nothing in America or Europe is worthy of emulation. Better to avoid Western corruption and hypocrisy, and then to do everything necessary to corrupt the West. In the meantime, true change in Russia is impossible. And anyway, there is no better alternative.

The factual world disappears amidst the proclamation of Russian innocence. Myth is universalized. Language loses meaning. The invasion of Ukraine never occurred, but if it did, then America provoked it. If Russia invaded, or didn't invade, it was to protect innocent Russians who were asking and not asking for Russian intervention. The logic of all this, says Timothy Snyder in *The Road to Unfreedom*, was that if Russia could not close the technological gap by becoming stronger, then it would try to make everybody else weaker: which meant keeping Ukraine away from America and Europe. And it meant also an information war, or a disinformation war, an intrusion into electoral contests in the West. The use of Western social media to launch disinformation: to divide, to lie, to distort. The winner loses less than the others, doesn't go as far into retreat. And the way forward for Russia is to disrupt alliances, to disrupt trade, to promote nationalist rhetoric and nationalist political parties. The message has a demonic clarity to it. All leaders and media lie to people everywhere; distrust is everywhere. Institutions are rigged. All of this has just enough truth to immobilize everybody.

Nationalists in America and Europe argued that Ukrainian protests on Maidan Square were inspired by the West, which wanted to reignite the Cold War. Conspiracy theories blaming the West were crafted by, among others, Marine Le Pen, Polish neo-fascist Mateusz Piskorski, Heinz-Christian Strache, leader of Austria's *Freiheitliche* party, and even Ron Paul, who defended the right of Russia to wage war abroad, although in American contexts he has consistently preached libertarianism or the right of the individual against the "intrusion" of state authority.

The link to the US should by now be obvious. The magic of Russia's propaganda machine has worked well, certainly better than could have been anticipated. In July 2016, Donald Trump proclaimed confidently: "Putin is not going into Ukraine, you can mark it down." It was not unusual for Trump to be wrong, after all he had internalized what Russia had once been fed on *First Kanal*. In fact, the invasion of Ukraine had begun more than 2 years previously, in February 2014, soon after snipers had murdered Ukrainians on Maidan Square. In a story straight out of John Le Carré, Trump was oddly connected to those events. In fact, it was not ignorance that led to his confidence about Russian innocence, though there was enough of the former to go around. The events in Ukraine helped provide Trump with his campaign manager, Paul Manafort, who worked as an assistant for the Ukrainian president, Viktor Yanukovych, in 2014. It was Manafort who briefed Trump about the Russian invasion that year. In 2016 this fact was inconvenient: so Trump wiped out the invasion altogether. It occurred, but it never actually occurred. The past disappeared: it was the end of history.

The magical cosmos of Putin squared nicely with the magical cosmos of Trump. Invasions could both occur and not occur. In 2016, the negotiations for Trump Tower in Moscow occurred, but they never occurred. They never occurred, but Trump stopped the negotiations in 2016.

As for Putin, he was an honest man who would never lie, insisted Trump, even if he did lie about the invasion of Ukraine. On June 9, 2016, a clandestine meeting in Trump Tower was held involving Donald Trump Jr., Paul Manafort, Jared Kushner, Natalia Veselnitskaya, a Russian lawyer, and several Russian operatives. Trump Jr. sought the meeting because Veselnitskaya and company had information, they said, which could help discredit Hillary Clinton and win the election for Trump Sr. Afterwards, President Trump said the meeting never occurred, but if it had occurred it had nothing to do with the presidential election: the discussion was about the adoption of Russian children.

Such was the swamp of American democracy. The Trump magical universe was a replica of the Putin magical world. A world where lies are truth, where what is true today becomes false tomorrow. A world, moreover, beyond good and evil, a kleptocratic world in which "uncertainty gives hope. Faith. Love." "Nothing is True: Everything is Possible."

There are lessons here. We are more like Russia than we think. We are not quite a kleptocracy, but in 2007 we showed signs of being on our way. We are not yet an autocracy, but Trump has succeeded in packing the Supreme Court with several justices possibly willing to do his bidding: and he has used his presidency to bribe the President of Ukraine to provide evidence of corruption of a political opponent, then refusing to acknowledge the authority of the House of Representatives for challenging his abuse of power. We are not yet a one-party state, but we are currently governed by a minority party that seeks to retain power indefinitely — regardless of the price. We are not yet a police state, but we have done little to stop the militarization of the police. We have not yet engaged in ethnic cleansing, but politicians at the highest level think nothing of stigmatizing immigrants and minorities for political advantage. We are not yet a fascist state, but we are standing in the doorway.

Which is why it is critical to maintain vigilance. To avoid distractions. To focus on what each of us can do. To find others like ourselves. To show up in public. The less we do, the more we resemble Russia.

Chapter 16

The Future: It is Our Collective Responsibility

William Faulkner once said that we live in an era when "the past is never dead, it is not even past." An era, moreover, of weakness, conformity, and a lack of significant leadership to overcome them. One consequence is that Americans have failed to realize how relative their thinking and judgments are — and how much they have succumbed to the myth of inevitability, as Timothy Snyder put it in *The Road to Unfreedom*. Decades earlier, Czeslaw Milosz presciently anticipated the conformity and politics of inevitability in *The Captive Mind*: "Man is so plastic a being that one can even conceive of the day when a thoroughly self-respecting citizen will crawl about on all fours, sporting a tail of brightly colored feathers as a sign of conformity to the order he lives in."

Anybody who has traveled to contemporary Russia or for that matter to contemporary Hungary, Poland, Israel, or Turkey will easily understand the warnings of Milosz. In the present context, we can add America, also, which has succumbed to the current rhetoric of hatred and demagoguery. Again, as Milosz adds, those struggling in adversity will be taught to expect that this also is the politics of inevitability: *"If something exists in one place, it will exist everywhere."* (Italics Milosz). If there are problems in Russia, they will soon appear in America. And as we know, if they don't appear "inevitably," then Vladimir Putin will know how to help them appear everywhere. Or, as Milosz put it, as early as 1946 in the "Child of Europe," written in New York:

Do not mention force, or you will be accused
Of upholding fallen doctrines in secret.

He who has power, has it by historical logic.
Respectfully bow to that logic...
Learn to predict a fire with unerring precision.
Then burn the house down to fulfill the prediction

Meant as a warning to those who predicted the future (Stalinism for example), and then used their power to fulfill their "prediction," the warning now stands as sentinel to what is happening in Donald Trump's America. Promise the wall between America and Mexico, then hold the country at ransom until the wall is built. Attempt to bribe a president of another country to help smear a political opponent, and when caught deny a bribe was made. Accuse the press of promoting fake news, any time that the press refuses to promote the opinions of the president, who often predicts fires and then ignites them (closing the government down, and then blaming others).

Warnings about the politics of inevitability have been there for decades. As Bernard Berenson put it: "I believe less and less in these dangerous dogmas...which make us accept whatever happens as irresistible and foolhardy to oppose." Shakespeare, in *Julius Caesar*, sounds an ominous (and similar) warning, "The fault, dear Brutus, is not in our stars, but in ourselves." To which T. S. Eliot adds, "Those vast impersonal forces," a chant always of scoundrels seeking refuge from their own acts dressed up in a wooly past.

A past that has now caught up to the present. For it was at the end of the decade of the 1980s that Francis Fukuyama made his fanciful prediction, or rather conclusion, that history was at an end, basing his idea on no less an authority than Georg Wilhelm von Hegel, the same who had inspired Marx and later Lenin and Stalin. Hegel had decided that the Prussian state would bring Germans to the promised land. Fukuyama, not one to see Prussia/ Germany as the historical endpoint, nevertheless stood history and the past on its head by proclaiming that liberal democracy was both triumphant and universally desirable. He meant that America had perfected institutions that somehow resembled what the entire world had always wanted — or should have wanted, and was belatedly succeeding in becoming. The future will look like the present, and it is good.

In fact, Fukuyama was repeating the same mistake made by Lenin, Stalin, and Gorbachev. They all believed, more or less, that communism was the future of the world. It would mean the perfection of human institutions and a kind of "end of history" of its own. And like them, Fukuyama set his eyes on the inevitable and desirable future. After all, there were now no alternatives, communism and fascism had both failed. The past had disappeared. And with no past, history had ended.

Shortly after Fukuyama celebrated the end of history, it began again.

Fragile borders, waves of immigrants and migrants exiting from failed states, endemic wars, economic dislocation, ethnic strife, shuffling of alliances, financial meltdown, unprecedented inequality, nationalist populist movements accompanied by authoritarian leaders and would-be dictators, challenges to both liberalism and democracy, historical atavism and reversions.

Again, the counsel of Czeslaw Milosz: "The living owe it to those who no longer can speak to tell their story for them." We all have a responsibility to the past, and to the victims of that past, to make our own history, and that in turn means not succumbing to the politics of inevitability or to the illusion that it is ultimately the same everywhere. And especially the illusion that the inevitable future will be exactly like the present. "The voice of passion," adds Milosz, "is better than the voice of reason. The passionless cannot change history."

But change it to what? And from what? What cannot be said often enough is that liberal democracy in America, as elsewhere, has ceased to be as liberal as it was, and is far less democratic than it needs to be. The liberal democracy that Fukuyama attempted to transform into eternity — and globally — has itself been blasted into the furnace of temporality. It has proven far more liquid than had been supposed. In a word, the US, the UK, and increasingly much of Western Europe and beyond, have failed to balance equality and liberty equitably. It can no longer be taken for granted that historic levels of inequality will not shortchange the liberty of many — possibly a majority of people in societies that have concentrated immense sums of wealth in the hands of narrow elites. Without a prophylactic state that protects citizens from the excesses of the free market, liberty will become a privilege, not a right. And when liberty shrinks, so will democracy in any meaningful sense. The result is what we have, post-democracy, in which the privileged few use the shell of democracy to limit, suspend or "abolish" democracy for the rest of us. It is worth remembering that a free people must be sovereign; a sovereign people must be democratic; and a democratic people can only be free if they are also relatively equal. Above all, we should remember that neoliberalism is a policy — one that benefits the few — as well as an ideology, and that the West was financially and economically strong previously, and more equal, based on widely embraced liberal and social democratic values.

We are back to Orwell. Free competition, the free market, "means for the great mass of people a tyranny probably worse, because more irresponsible, than that of the state. The trouble with competitions is that somebody wins them." Historically, Orwell reminds us, "that is where it (free competition) has led, and since the vast majority of people would far rather have State regimentation than slumps and unemployment, the drift towards collectivism is bound to continue if popular opinion has any say in the matter."

The tyranny of the (globalized) market has led to monopoly, and then to slumps and then to unemployment and poverty: and then to the breeding grounds of instability, fear, and (often) the emergence of a tyrant promising to punish market winners (which never happens). The "free market" can also be a kind of politics of eternity, to repeat that phrase again. For it is no longer possible to pretend that democracy can thrive when the free market — liberty for some — has the potential to destroy the planet for all, or to divide us (eternally) into tribes of haves and have-nots. When the liberty of a few comes at the expense of the liberty of the many, tyranny ("inevitably") will be hovering nearby. At that point we will be living in post-democracy, and we may not even be aware of it. We are in fact already there.

We have learned that there is no exit from history. Attempted exits in the past have ended in the gulag, or in genocide, or in war. Whether looking to a realm of freedom at the end of history, a utopia of virtue and selflessness, or humanity living in universal harmony without class or clan, or searching for the purity of a golden age that never actually occurred — an earlier attempted exit from history — humanity has never quite succeeded. There has never been a restoration of a perfect past, nor an exit into a golden future.

Neither has the cybernetic revolution produced an exit from history. Technology promises liberation and is equated with Progress by the sellers of modernity. But the globalization that it helps produce does not emancipate us. Instead, it widens the gap between the rich and the poor, the powerful and the weak, the educated and those poorly educated. And it pollutes the environment before there is the will or the means to protect it. It promises the world, but only delivers it to those who can afford it.

Finally, I should like to cite some words I wrote more than a decade ago in *The Revenge of History* when the world we have inherited was just coming into focus. This is a warning against the promise that technology will save us. And it is a remembrance of things past, a hope of things yet to come:

The cybernetic revolution abolishes the old world, and heralds the new. Champions of the brave new world argue that the old world is obsolete, inefficient, irrelevant and undesirable. The past is repudiated, recreated, or remembered only by antiquarians, historians, or the elderly who are besieged by nostalgia. Sometimes the poor and even the middle classes are gripped by anxiety about a future in which they are likely to be more marginal, redundant and forgotten than in the visibly receding past. But the more things change, the more unrecognizable is the present. The world comes to resemble the past: out of control, insecure, hostile, and abounding in tribal hatreds, class struggles, populations of refugees in eternal flight, new struggles for self-determination by people trapped behind borders they never made, ancient rivalries of faith.

The cybernetic revolution and globalization have eroded the benchmarks and borders of history, community, nation, and state. They have introduced a blur of obsolescence, mobility, change, and innovation. The world and its peoples, and their ideas and faiths, all become nomadic. The gaps, the borders between peoples and faiths and politics, are increasingly penetrated by would-be dictators, authoritarian humbugs, who ply new promises of national greatness, who promote new exits from history, who preach America First, who weave new myths of a golden past, who build walls against imagined enemies, who cynically dispose of our institutions, who challenge the frontiers of our constitution while packing courts to compromise and limit it. Who deny truth by inventing alternative facts (and alternative histories).

No people can be free if they are seduced by alternative facts. Democracy fails when politicians use disinformation campaigns and then accuse their critics of promoting fake news. Warnings were uttered as early as the eighteenth century. "If a nation expects to be ignorant and free," said Thomas Jefferson, "it expects what never was and never will be...The people cannot be safe without information. Where the press is free, and every man able to read, all is safe."

Having forgotten the past, we are now repeating it. We are descending toward chaos if not into barbarism once again, only some 8 decades since the Third Reich came to power and put the entire planet in peril. As Richard Evans reminds us in his book *In Hitler's Shadow*, "[The Third Reich] stands as a dreadful warning of the destructive potential of technology. It shows the ultimate consequences of racism...The Third Reich's bureaucratic deformation of language, its exaltation of ideological fanaticism, its cult of unthinking obedience to orders," stand as warning to all ages of how democracy can disappear overnight. And how dangerous nationalism can be because it divides us into tribes. It should not be forgotten that the vast majority of Germans supported or tolerated Hitler in 1938 — the year of Kristallnacht — and firmly identified with his policies. They abandoned democracy when they were seduced by the magical thought of Hitler.

It is to deny fictive Golden Ages that we must remember the real legacies of our past. It is to repel false visions of a perfect (utopian) future that we must protect our liberties in the present. And we must acknowledge that to do this, we must resist the corruption of language, we must resolve to speak truth to power, we must reject unthinking obedience, we must contradict what we know to be false, and we must resist dividing ourselves into tribes.

We must all be accountable in the present. History, of the past, for the present and future, is our collective responsibility. Otherwise we will be stuck with authoritarian leaders acting as our proxies for a future that will benefit few of us.

About the Author

Jack Luzkow is professor of history at Fontbonne University. He is the author of *The Revenge of History: Why the Past Endures*; *A Critique of Francis Fukuyama, What's Left? Marxism, Utopianism and the Revolt Against History*; *The Great Forgetting: The Past, Present and Future of Social Democracy and the Welfare State*; and *Monopoly Restored: How the Super-Rich Robbed Main Street*.

In *Monopoly Restored*, Professor Luzkow argued that much wealth has been based on inheritance, tax evasion, political influence, and wage theft. The super-rich of today derives its income from ownership or control of scarce assets, or assets artificially made scarce, including patents, monopolies, and subsidies. Luzkow has been interviewed on NPR a number of times. Ralph Nader has interviewed him for the *Ralph Nader Radio Hour,* and he has been interviewed by Joe Donahue at WAMC, an NPR outlet. Professor Luzkow maintains a blog at jackluzkow.com, where he writes about current politics and their historical background, and a number of topics related to his books, including the past and present of democracy. He plans to launch an oral history, for people living in Britain and the US, especially the working classes, to tell their stories since the great meltdown called the Great Recession back in 2008. For further details please go to jackluzkow.com.

Ralph Nader had this to say about Professor Luzkow's previous work, *Monopoly Restored*: "Jack Luzkow's meticulous roadmap shows that the power of the few plutocrats over the many citizens produces unmerited wealth that mostly belongs to the people. That's enough to motivate taking it back for mass well-being and civic self-respect." If you agree, let me hear your story!

CULTURE, SOCIETY & POLITICS

The modern world is at an impasse. Disasters scroll across our smartphone screens and we're invited to like, follow or upvote, but critical thinking is harder and harder to find. Rather than connecting us in common struggle and debate, the internet has sped up and deepened a long-standing process of alienation and atomization. Zer0 Books wants to work against this trend. With critical theory as our jumping off point, we aim to publish books that make our readers uncomfortable. We want to move beyond received opinions.

Zer0 Books is on the left and wants to reinvent the left. We are sick of the injustice, the suffering and the stupidity that defines both our political and cultural world, and we aim to find a new foundation for a new struggle.

If this book has helped you to clarify an idea, solve a problem or extend your knowledge, you may want to check out our online content as well. Look for Zer0 Books: Advancing Conversations in the iTunes directory and for our Zer0 Books YouTube channel.

Popular videos include:

Žižek and the Double Blackmain

The Intellectual Dark Web is a Bad Sign

Can there be an Anti-SJW Left?

Answering Jordan Peterson on Marxism

Follow us on Facebook
at https://www.facebook.com/ZeroBooks and Twitter at https://
twitter.com/Zer0Books

Bestsellers from Zer0 Books include:

Give Them An Argument
Logic for the Left
Ben Burgis
Many serious leftists have learned to distrust talk of logic. This is
a serious mistake.
Paperback: 978-1-78904-210-8 ebook: 978-1-78904-211-5

Poor but Sexy
Culture Clashes in Europe East and West
Agata Pyzik
How the East stayed East and the West stayed West.
Paperback: 978-1-78099-394-2 ebook: 978-1-78099-395-9

An Anthropology of Nothing in Particular
Martin Demant Frederiksen
A journey into the social lives of meaninglessness.
Paperback: 978-1-78535-699-5 ebook: 978-1-78535-700-8

In the Dust of This Planet
Horror of Philosophy vol. 1
Eugene Thacker
In the first of a series of three books on the Horror of Philosophy,
In the Dust of This Planet offers the genre of horror as a way of
thinking about the unthinkable.
Paperback: 978-1-84694-676-9 ebook: 978-1-78099-010-1

The End of Oulipo?
An Attempt to Exhaust a Movement
Lauren Elkin, Veronica Esposito
Paperback: 978-1-78099-655-4 ebook: 978-1-78099-656-1

Capitalist Realism
Is There No Alternative?
Mark Fisher
An analysis of the ways in which capitalism has presented itself
as the only realistic political-economic system.
Paperback: 978-1-84694-317-1 ebook: 978-1-78099-734-6

Rebel Rebel
Chris O'Leary
David Bowie: every single song. Everything you want to know,
everything you didn't know.
Paperback: 978-1-78099-244-0 ebook: 978-1-78099-713-1

Kill All Normies
Angela Nagle
Online culture wars from 4chan and Tumblr to Trump.
Paperback: 978-1- 78535-543-1 ebook: 978-1-78535-544-8

Cartographies of the Absolute
Alberto Toscano, Jeff Kinkle
An aesthetics of the economy for the twenty-first century.
Paperback: 978-1-78099-275-4 ebook: 978-1-78279-973-3

Malign Velocities
Accelerationism and Capitalism
Benjamin Noys
Long listed for the Bread and Roses Prize 2015, *Malign Velocities*
argues against the need for speed, tracking acceleration
as the symptom of the ongoing crises of capitalism.
Paperback: 978-1-78279-300-7 ebook: 978-1-78279-299-4

Meat Market
Female Flesh under Capitalism
Laurie Penny
A feminist dissection of women's bodies as the fleshy fulcrum of
capitalist cannibalism, whereby women are both consumers and
consumed.
Paperback: 978-1-84694-521-2 ebook: 978-1-84694-782-7

Babbling Corpse
Vaporwave and the Commodification of Ghosts
Grafton Tanner
Paperback: 978-1-78279-759-3 ebook: 978-1-78279-760-9

New Work New Culture
Work we want and a culture that strengthens us
Frithjoff Bergmann
A serious alternative for mankind and the planet.
Paperback: 978-1-78904-064-7 ebook: 978-1-78904-065-4